September–Decen

Day by Day
with
God

Rooting women's lives in the Bible

The Bible Reading Fellowship
15 The Chambers, Vineyard
Abingdon OX14 3FE
brf.org.uk

The Bible Reading Fellowship (BRF) is a Registered Charity (233280)

ISBN 978 0 85746 781 2
All rights reserved

This edition © 2019 The Bible Reading Fellowship
Cover image © Getty images

Distributed in Australia by:
MediaCom Education Inc, PO Box 610, Unley, SA 5061
Tel: 1 800 811 311 | admin@mediacom.org.au

Distributed in New Zealand by:
Scripture Union Wholesale, PO Box 760, Wellington
Tel: 04 385 0421 | suwholesale@clear.net.nz

Acknowledgements

Scripture quotations marked NIV taken from The Holy Bible, New International Version (Anglicised edition) copyright © 1979, 1984, 2011 by Biblica. Used by permission of Hodder & Stoughton Publishers, a Hachette UK company. All rights reserved. 'NIV' is a registered trademark of Biblica. UK trademark number 1448790.

Scripture quotations marked NLT taken from the Holy Bible, New Living Translation, copyright © 1996, 2004, 2007, 2013. Used by permission of Tyndale House Publishers, Inc., Carol Stream, Illinois 60188. All rights reserved.

Scripture quotations marked NCV taken from the New Century Version®. Copyright © 2005 by Thomas Nelson. Used by permission. All rights reserved.

Scripture quotations marked MSG taken from The Message, copyright © 1993, 1994, 1995, 1996, 2000, 2001, 2002 by Eugene H. Peterson. Used by permission of NavPress. All rights reserved. Represented by Tyndale House Publishers, Inc.

Scripture quotations marked AMP taken from the Amplified® Bible, Copyright © 2015 by The Lockman Foundation. Used by permission. Lockman.org

Scripture quotations marked TPT taken from The Passion Translation®. Copyright © 2017 by BroadStreet Publishing® Group, LLC. Used by permission. All rights reserved. thePassionTranslation.com

Scripture quotations marked ESV taken from the Holy Bible, English Standard Version Anglicised, published by HarperCollins Publishers, © 2001 Crossway Bibles, a division of Good News Publishers. Used by permission. All rights reserved.

Every effort has been made to trace and contact copyright owners for material used in this resource. We apologise for any inadvertent omissions or errors, and would ask those concerned to contact us so that full acknowledgement can be made in the future.

A catalogue record for this book is available from the British Library

Printed by Gutenberg Press, Tarxien, Malta

Day by Day
with
God

Edited by **Ali Herbert** and **Jill Rattle**   **September–December 2019**

Writers in this issue

Amy Boucher Pye is a writer and speaker who runs the *Woman Alive* book club. She's the author of the award-winning *Finding Myself in Britain* (Authentic, 2015) and *The Living Cross* (BRF, 2016). Find her at **amyboucherpye.com**.

Michele D. Morrison is working on her bucket list, babysitting grandchildren, aiding her nonagenarian mother in California, as well as editing the church magazine. She writes and blogs at **tearsamidthealiencorn.blogspot.com**.

Rachel Turner is the Parenting for Faith Pioneer at BRF (**parentingforfaith. org**). Over the past 15 years, she has worked across a variety of denominations as a children's, youth and family life pastor. She is the author of five books.

Diana Archer is an educator, writer and speaker with a theological background. She founded the charity tastelifeuk (**tastelifeuk.org**), which trains people to offer hope and tools for recovery for those with eating disorders.

Christine Platt lives in New Zealand and enjoys the freedom and opportunities that retirement brings. As well as encouraging mission in her church, she also teaches English to Chinese people and to young people in East Timor.

Lyndall Bywater is a freelance writer, trainer and consultant in all things prayer. She has a passion to help people get to know God better and is the author of *Faith in the Making* (BRF, 2018) and *Prayer in the Making* (BRF, 2019).

Helen Williams has worked in music, education, management consultancy and administration. She currently finds herself alongside her husband, an Anglican bishop, in some extraordinarily diverse contexts, while continuing to work as an accompanist.

Victoria Byrne is the Seniors Pastor at St Stephen's Church, Twickenham, working with older people. She is co-author of *Hope & Spice*, an Indian cookbook with authentic recipes and stories of transformation from Delhi's slums, raising funds for Asha India.

Hannah Fytche read Theology at Cambridge University. She's passionate about seeing God's love transform lives and communities, and embraces this passion through writing, speaking and spending time with friends and family.

Selina Stone is Tutor and Lecturer in Political Theology at St Mellitus College. She is also a part-time PhD student at the University of Birmingham, her home city, researching liberation and justice in Pentecostal theology and ministry.

Jill Rattle and Ali Herbert write...

Jill: Celebrating a special anniversary, we invited people from seven neighbouring houses to join us. They came – Chinese, Indian, Jamaican, Irish, Polish, English and Filipino. It was just brilliant! I am amazed at the diversity of women, men and children God has lovingly created. What riches!

There may not be quite the same cultural spread among our wonderful contributors but there is such diversity in their styles, their approaches and, above all, their encounter with God in his scriptures that makes every issue so rich. Sometimes, as editor, I worry that the chosen passages will overlap or the commentaries will be too similar. But, do you know, I think we could have ten women writing on the same passage and each would bring something different. And you, the reader, would receive each note differently. That is because each of us has a unique relationship with God, and the Holy Spirit is our personal tutor, teaching us one by one. No wonder Michele D. Morrison entitles her notes on Psalm 119 'The treasure of scripture'. What riches!

Ali: We are really pleased to introduce you to two new writers in this issue. Selina Stone is a lecturer at St Mellitus theological college and was born and raised in Birmingham. She has a particular passion for social and political justice and in these notes is taking us through the story of hope in Luke's gospel account of the birth of Jesus. Hannah Fytche is our other new contributor: she has published a book with BRF for young women called *God's Daughters* (BRF, 2016), looking at some of the pressures we can experience and the way in which God pours out his love and grace on us. She also has a newer book out, *Rooted in God's Grace* (BRF, 2018). In these notes, Hannah is exploring the book of Ruth and showing how, through an ancient Hebrew story, we can discover the truth of God's love for us and find again the courage to take those everyday steps to keep following him. Hannah encourages us to hear the whisper of the Father's voice to us in the busyness of our lives and, as we begin this autumn term of notes, we hope to encourage you to keep listening out, every day, for God's loving whisper to you.

Obedience and deliverance: Exodus

Amy Boucher Pye writes:

September seems a time for new beginnings, with social media feeds brimming with smile-inducing photos of cute kids in their fresh school uniforms, ready for their first days of school. The nights start to arrive sooner, and we might begin to think about the Advent and Christmas seasons, in that sort of far-off sense of not having to take them too seriously just yet. As we get back to routine after the summer holidays, it can be a good time to delve into some fresh Bible reading notes. This month, we start off by looking at the life of Moses.

What do you think of when you consider this man? Perhaps an image from an old movie will flash into your mind, with Moses of the long grey beard smashing the tablets of the ten commandments in fury. Or him, again in technicolour, glancing back over his shoulder at the Egyptians as the Red Sea splashes over them.

I used to think of him like that but, having studied the book of Exodus a bit more, I now think of Moses as a man not eager to become a leader! He tries so many different ways to escape leading God's people, not realising that he only has to say 'Yes' to one step at a time, for God will equip him moment by moment. And this is what happens – through the trials and plagues and hardships of leaving Egypt and wandering in the desert, Moses' faith in God grows and flourishes. He comes to believe strongly that God will follow through on his promises.

These days, I think of Moses as a man who isn't perfect, but who is a 'good enough' leader. He has to learn that his leadership resources are enough only if he has God by his side.

Whatever struggles or challenges we face, we too can cling to this truth. God wants us to be his people, and is with us always when we welcome him into our lives. We can trust him all our days, from the big decisions to the minutiae of the moment.

I pray your faith will be strengthened as you see how God moved in the lives of the Israelites thousands of years ago.

God rules

Then a new king, to whom Joseph meant nothing, came to power in Egypt. 'Look,' he said to his people, 'the Israelites have become far too numerous for us. Come, we must deal shrewdly with them or they will become even more numerous.' (NIV)

'They took all the "W" keys!' exclaimed a White House staffer.

That's what I heard on the Washington D.C. grapevine, just after a regime change from one political party to another following a presidential election. Some who served the Clinton administration, as a parting prank, left altered keyboards for those working for the new president, George W. Bush.

After Joseph died, the Israelites faced far worse from the king who came to power in Egypt. Having no personal links to Joseph and his brothers, the new ruler implemented oppressive measures on God's people, forcing them to labour under harsh conditions. But something surprising happened – God helped them to prosper: 'the more they were oppressed, the more they multiplied and spread' (v. 12). In God's world, rulers are mere mortals who hold only limited power, whether or not they realise it.

And this is a major theme in the first part of the book of Exodus, acted out in the relationship between Pharaoh and the Israelites, who are led by Moses. Pharaoh doesn't want to lose the slave labour he enjoys through God's people; nor does he want to acknowledge the Lord as God. But the unrelenting plagues will eventually reveal who is the ruler to be followed – God.

In times of political turmoil, we might be tempted to despair. But reading through the book of Exodus can act as a corrective to our turbulent emotions. It can help us to remember that God is God and that although we may suffer through the foibles of our leaders, he will never leave us. We can cry out to him for help, even as Moses did for the Israelites. And God will hear us.

Creator God, may we turn to you as the one who set the universe into order. Please bring peace and healing to the areas in the world torn with conflict.

AMY BOUCHER PYE

Exile

When Pharaoh heard of this, he tried to kill Moses, but Moses fled from Pharaoh and went to live in Midian. (NIV)

My children are experts in spotting hypocrisy or inconsistency in me, especially if I treat them differently, however unintentionally. How quickly they point out this behaviour that is unacceptable to them!

Moses experienced something similar, but on a bigger scale. Thinking that no one was watching, he killed an Egyptian who was beating a Hebrew. Perhaps, in defending the oppressed Israelite, he was trying to throw off his identity as the son of Pharaoh's daughter, who rescued him from the River Nile (see Exodus 2:1–10). He's commended in the book of Hebrews for eschewing this identity, although not for his actions here (see Hebrews 11:24). We aren't told in the Exodus account the exact circumstances of the killing, but he was clearly acting rashly and without God's prompting.

Moses' murderous actions propel him to become a foreigner in a strange land as he flees Egypt to live in Midian, where he marries Zipporah. While he's away from Egypt, the king dies and the Israelites continue to cry out against the oppression they experience. God hears their pleas and remembers his covenant with the Israelite forefathers. Perhaps the Lord used this time of exile to protect Moses, preparing him to be a reluctant leader.

When we do wrong, we often have to face the consequences of our sins, as Moses did. But we can look to God for forgiveness and restoration, seeking his wisdom on how we can live in a way that brings glory to him. We can ask him to give us an undivided heart and joined-up actions, which reflect our desire to honour him. Although this side of heaven we'll continue to fail and fall into sin, we know that our loving Father will help us to do so less and less as we journey with him.

Loving Father, I'm sorry for the ways I fail you and others. Soften my heart, that I might confess my wrongdoing and receive your forgiveness. Make me malleable in your hands.

AMY BOUCHER PYE

A crisis of confidence

But Moses said to God, 'Who am I that I should go to Pharaoh and bring the Israelites out of Egypt?' And God said, 'I will be with you.' (NIV)

I remember clearly the day I walked into impressive offices in Hammersmith, London, to become a senior editor with HarperCollins. I'd never before worked for a big corporation, and thus felt distinctly awed. Heart pounding, I entered through the security area and made my way up to the fourth floor to take up my new position. Although I felt out of my depth, I knew that God was with me, and that he'd given me wonderful colleagues to help me find my way.

Moses may have had an auspicious upbringing in Pharaoh's court, but he seemed content to leave all of that behind and embrace the life of shepherding his father-in-law's flock in Midian. But now he is 80, and all of that changes when he's visited by an angel of the Lord with a new commission – to lead God's people out of slavery. His instant response, however, is, 'Who, me?' He feels unfit for leadership, and not at all sure that he wants this new role. But God assures him that he is God and that he won't leave him. The Lord renews the covenant he made with Abraham, Isaac and Jacob, and promises Moses that he will indeed lead his people out of Egypt.

My job as senior editor pales in comparison to Moses' grand commission from God. But God will often call us out of our comfort zones to serve him in what may feel like audacious ways. We might squeak out our concerns of why we're not equipped, and he'll remind us that we have all of the resources we need, for he will be with us.

How have you experienced God's call? What new venture might he be beckoning you to embrace?

Lord of all, remind me of your loving presence, and equip me for the many things you're calling me to do. Please help me and never leave me.

AMY BOUCHER PYE

Cycle of blame

'Let my people go, so that they may hold a festival to me in the wilderness.' Pharaoh said, 'Who is the Lord, that I should obey him and let Israel go? I do not know the Lord and I will not let Israel go.' (NIV)

Today's passage marks the beginning of the conflict between Pharaoh and Moses, with Moses asking the leader of the Egyptians to release them to worship God and Pharaoh not bending his will. Pharaoh's response is telling, for it highlights the nature of the battle – that he doesn't acknowledge the Lord as God. Instead, he strengthens his resolve to keep his workforce in place and makes their tasks even more difficult by not providing straw for the bricks they must make.

Part of what I find interesting here is the cycle of blame and finger-pointing. Ever since Adam took the fruit from Eve and explained his actions to God as 'she made me do it' (see Genesis 3:12), people try to escape the consequences of their actions. Here, when Pharaoh clamps down on God's people, they blame Moses. Moses listens to their grumbling and in turn tells God that the Lord has brought trouble on his people. Does God get frustrated with their lack of faith? No. Instead, he reassures Moses, and therefore the people, that he is working through Pharaoh and will deliver them from this oppression. The Lord sees the whole picture, unlike his people.

When we experience times of darkness and disappointment, we may question why God would allow us to hurt so much. When we pray to him, we may sense silence. But although we may not feel his presence, we can believe the promises we find in the Bible, such as Moses received: 'Now you will see what I will do' (6:1). We may have to wait for God to act, but we can trust that, because he loves us so much, he will help us to walk through the difficult times.

Lord, reassure me of your presence when you feel so far from me. As I follow you, help me to lean on what I know to be true from your promises in the Bible.

AMY BOUCHER PYE

Rivers of blood

'This is what the Lord says: by this you will know that I am the Lord: with the staff that is in my hand I will strike the water of the Nile, and it will be changed into blood.' (NIV)

Moses is a reluctant leader, not eager to take on God's great plan to release the Israelites from bondage in Egypt. But he agrees, even though at times he still doubts his calling and capability despite God allowing his brother Aaron to speak for him. As Moses leads the people, step by step, his trust in God grows – for time after time, the Lord delivers. Ten times Moses tells Pharaoh, 'Let my people go.' And ten times the Egyptian leader responds negatively, which results in pain and destruction.

First, as we read today, Moses turns the river to blood, which the Egyptian magicians can also do. Then comes the plague of frogs, which again the magicians replicate. But they cannot enact any of the other plagues – the gnats, flies, livestock, boils, hail, locusts and darkness that all rain down on the Egyptians. Each time, Moses tells Pharaoh to follow God and let the Israelites go. But each time, God hardens Pharaoh's heart, and he does not relent.

Not only does Pharaoh learn of God's majesty, but so do Moses and the Israelites. Through each manifestation of God's power, Moses sees that he can put his trust in him, for God is faithful. As a result, Moses becomes a strong leader of God's people.

We don't live in the special time of Moses, and so I don't expect God to be sending plagues to get our attention. Instead, more amazingly, we have the revelation of the Bible and the active presence of Jesus and the Holy Spirit in our lives. May we serve the triune God with wonder and thanks, knowing that we, like Moses, can trust him.

Father God, I ache to see so much pain in the world, sometimes caused by natural disasters. Through your mercy, please bring healing and help.

AMY BOUCHER PYE

Mass exodus

During the night Pharaoh summoned Moses and Aaron and said, 'Up! Leave my people, you and the Israelites! Go, worship the Lord as you have requested. Take your flocks and herds, as you have said, and go. And also bless me.' (NIV)

After the horrors of the nine plagues, still Pharaoh will not relent and let the Israelites go. And so comes the final, dreadful plague – that of the killing of the firstborn in families and in their livestock. The Lord gives his people precautions that will keep them from the angel of death – they will be passed over because of the mark of blood on their doorframes. This passing over and their leaving of Egypt will thereafter be marked by their biggest act of remembrance in the year: the Passover.

This exodus is massive; biblical commentators believe that the six hundred thousand men mentioned in verse 37 means all together, with women and children, two or three million people – plus livestock and the goods given to the people by the Egyptians. The Israelites number as many people as the Egyptians and are far more numerous than those living in Canaan, the promised land. We can understand why Pharaoh doesn't want to give up all of this free labour.

With the spectre of death everywhere, Pharaoh finally acquiesces to Moses' request, even in his pain asking for Moses to bless him. And so God's people escape the bondage of slavery in Egypt, free to serve their God and to flourish. What could possibly go wrong? As we'll see, rather a lot.

As we ponder the death of the firstborn, which secured freedom for others, let's consider the New Testament links. Our Father God didn't spare his only Son, Jesus, but sent him to die in our place for our wrongdoing. He wasn't passed over. How grateful we are for that gift of freedom and redemption!

Lord, please deepen my gratefulness for the gift of salvation, for the freedom to live and serve you. May I somehow share news of this amazing grace with others today.

AMY BOUCHER PYE

Dry ground

Moses answered the people, 'Do not be afraid. Stand firm and you will see the deliverance the Lord will bring you today. The Egyptians you see today you will never see again. The Lord will fight for you; you need only to be still.' (NIV)

As I drove back to London from Devon, I stopped by the seaside to soak in the wonders of land, water, sunshine and fresh air. After walking along the shore, enjoying the birds, boats and buoys, I knew it was time to go home, so decided to cut across the foreshore (that area of the beach where the tide goes out). Being both a city girl and not a native Briton, I didn't realise just how muddy the foreshore could become. Soon my boots were stuck in the sludge, with me on the verge of falling. Only the removal of my boots, and a squelchy walk to shore in my socks, saved me from being completely covered in mud.

But the Israelites face no mucky silt to sink into when they cross the Red Sea. Instead, God gives them dry ground, in a wonderful miracle of the wind and waves. For although they have left Egypt, Pharaoh hasn't given up. Even though his firstborn perished, he regrets releasing his labour force. God knows this and has a plan to show not only Pharaoh that he's the only true God, but Moses and the Israelites too. For as the Egyptian armies bear down on the Israelites, God's people immediately start to complain and grumble to their leaders. Note, however, how Moses' faith has grown, for he assures the Israelites that God will deliver them (vv. 13–14). And God does so magnificently, using a strong wind at Moses' command to push back the water of the sea so that the Israelites can walk through on dry ground. He proves that he is the God of the wind and the waves, the one who fights on behalf of his people.

Lord of creation, you are mighty and powerful. Thank you for your unfailing love, and that you hold me up when I feel like I'm falling.

AMY BOUCHER PYE

Manna-burgers

The Lord said to Moses, 'I have heard the grumbling of the Israelites. Tell them, "At twilight you will eat meat, and in the morning you will be filled with bread. Then you will know that I am the Lord your God."'
(NIV)

When I was young, I loved listening to the songs of American song writer, Keith Green (find him on YouTube!). Even today, when I read the story of the Israelites receiving bread from heaven, I think of his song, 'So you wanna go back to Egypt'. In it, he outlines the miracles God grants through Moses to release his people, and yet how they bellyached over their lot in the desert. Their thirst and hunger soon drives them to cry out, 'If only we had died by the Lord's hand in Egypt!' (v. 3)

Keith Green's song reveals humorously the Israelites' fickleness. Even though God gives them meat at twilight and bread in the morning, they soon tire of this diet. The song lists some creative variants of manna: manna hotcakes, manna soufflé, manna waffles, manna burgers, manna bagels, filet of manna, manna patty and my favourite, ba-manna-bread. And yet the Israelites grumble – though, to be fair, they had to eat the stuff for 40 years.

But the bread from heaven teaches God's people – and, by extension, us – the importance of depending on God for our daily sustenance. Keeping bread for longer than we should will make it hard and mouldy. But only taking or making what is needed for the day – and sharing it round – means that the bread stays fresh and wholesome: fitting for our physical needs. And of course, as we feast on the Bread of Life, Jesus, we find that our spiritual needs are met daily too.

When is the last time you ate a piece of bread? Consider whether it was such an everyday affair that you don't remember it, or if it was unusual. How can you turn your physical eating of bread into a reminder to look to God for your needs?

'Our Father in heaven, hallowed be your name, your kingdom come, your will be done, on earth as it is in heaven. Give us today our daily bread'
(Matthew 6:9–11).

AMY BOUCHER PYE

New covenant

'You yourselves have seen what I did to Egypt, and how I carried you on eagles' wings and brought you to myself. Now if you obey me fully and keep my covenant, then out of all nations you will be my treasured possession.' (NIV)

In my late 20s, I yearned to be married. After a broken engagement, my desire for a husband became overwhelming, and finally I had to relinquish my hopes and dreams, for they were hindering my relationship with God. When I was single, I didn't realise that marriage, although delightful, would entail a different set of challenges and disappointments to singleness. After all, we live in a fallen world and will never reach a hoped-for utopia on earth. Instead, our longings will be fulfilled fully when we meet God in heaven, and in the meantime, he promises his presence with us.

Life in the desert involved drudgery and travel for the Israelites, but they were constantly dissatisfied and yearning for things to change. When they lived in Egypt, they sought release from slavery; then, when they were free but living in the desert, they desired to be settled in the promised land. The only way they could find peace was to honour and serve the living God.

The Lord calls Moses to the mountaintop to renew the covenant with him and the people. They will be God's 'treasured possession' if they obey him and keep his commands (v. 5). He will make them a 'kingdom of priests and a holy nation' (v. 6). This latter promise forms the kernel of the New Testament notion of the priesthood of all believers (1 Peter 2:5–9). No longer will only the priest act on our behalf, but we can enjoy a direct relationship with God: one that will help us fill those empty places that drive our longings, as I found in my 20s.

Can you turn to God in any areas of disappointment or need that you face today?

Lord God, through your Spirit, fill me with your love and grace. Help me to know that I am yours, and you are mine.

AMY BOUCHER PYE

A rule of life

And God spoke all these words: 'I am the Lord your God, who brought you out of Egypt, out of the land of slavery. You shall have no other gods before me.' (NIV)

When I first moved to England, touring the country and visiting many churches, I was surprised to see the ten commandments often featured in two panels at the front, usually alongside the Lord's Prayer and the Apostles' Creed. To me, the ten commandments seemed important but outdated, conjuring up 'thou's and 'thee's and 'shalt not's. But delving into the Old Testament over the years has brought me a deeper appreciation for God's laws. I see now how he gave them to his people so that they could remain pure in their devotion to him. His rules are for their flourishing, not a straitjacket to hinder them.

What strikes me especially about the ten commandments is how God starts off by telling his people to honour him above all else. Because he brought them out of slavery, saving them from serving other gods, he can demand their all. Living in Canaan, they will come into close contact with many other gods, such as those thought to increase fertility and to promote the growth of crops. And if they intermarry with the Canaanites, they will be tempted to dilute their allegiance to the one true God. All of this will be to their detriment, and so the Lord sets out these first key requirements.

How do we honour God in our lives? Do we give him our all? Or have we elevated our families above him? Our work? Our volunteering? Our relationships? Our leisure pursuits?

Spend some time today considering where your allegiance lies. If you feel the need to return to God, know that he welcomes you with open arms. Indeed, he runs towards you.

Father God, I want no other gods before you in my life. Help me to put you first in all the moments of my days.

AMY BOUCHER PYE

Gods of gold

Then the Lord said to Moses, 'Go down, because your people, whom you brought up out of Egypt, have become corrupt. They have been quick to turn away from what I commanded them and have made themselves an idol cast in the shape of a calf.' (NIV)

When Moses received the ten commandments and other laws from God, he shared them with the Israelites, and they responded with one voice: 'Everything the Lord has said we will do' (Exodus 24:3). It doesn't take them too long, however, to forget their commitment. When, in their minds, Moses takes too long on the mountaintop as he communicates with God, the people get restless. Making a persuasive case to Aaron, they convince him to lead them in breaking the second commandment. From worshiping the one true God, they quickly descend into honouring some gold formed into a calf.

As you read today's passage, note the exchange between Moses and God, and the power of prayer. With this latest betrayal, God says that he's done with his wayward people, wanting to rid himself of them and their wandering ways. But Moses pleads on their behalf, pointing out that if God smites them, it will be his name that suffers ill repute among his enemies. Why save them from the Egyptians just to wipe them out himself? And so God relents.

From this exchange, I see the mercy and love of God, for he responds to the cries of his people. We can't determine how he will answer our prayers, for he remains God and we are not. But we can appeal to his tender heart, praying on behalf of our loved ones and even for strangers and nations.

What big issues in the world weigh on you today? You might like to set aside some time to pray about one or two of these, perhaps with a friend, voicing your concerns to God. As Alfred Tennyson said, 'More things are wrought by prayer than this world dreams of.'

Lord, often we express our undivided commitment to you, only to find ourselves breaking those vows in little or big ways. Forgive us, and help us to stay true to you.

AMY BOUCHER PYE

Face to face

As Moses went into the tent, the pillar of cloud would come down and stay at the entrance, while the Lord spoke with Moses… The Lord would speak to Moses face to face, as one speaks to a friend. (NIV)

Those who are put off reading the Old Testament because of a perception of God's wrath within it would do well to read this story about the tent of meeting. Here, the creator of the universe makes himself available to Moses and the Israelites, speaking to Moses 'face to face' as to a friend (v. 11). The Lord welcomes any of the Israelites with concerns or questions to enquire of him. He is not a God far off, but a God near at hand. (This meeting tent is not the formal one – the tabernacle – of Exodus 25—31, but a similar place of meeting with God, created before Moses received detailed instructions.)

Through all that the Israelites experienced in leaving Egypt and the many miracles Moses performed on God's behalf in the wilderness, their faith in God becomes stronger. And now as they see the pillar of cloud outside the tent, they worship him, knowing that his presence is there.

With the coming of the Holy Spirit at Pentecost, we have the promise of God's presence with us at all times, tent or no tent. When we call on him, he is with us. He promises never to leave us. And he speaks to us as with a friend.

Cultivating a friendship with God isn't arduous, but we do need to dedicate time with him, reading his word, worshiping him and communicating with him. A walk through creation can foster times of contemplation, or perhaps you'll find closeness with God through fellowship with one or more fellow believers. I enjoy writing out my prayers to God, sometimes in the form of poetry, or taking time to walk along a running brook while praising God as creator. What ushers you into God's presence?

God of the ages, thank you for the gift of being with you. Help me not to take this privilege for granted, and strengthen my love for you.

AMY BOUCHER PYE

God's attributes

'The Lord, the Lord, the compassionate and gracious God, slow to anger, abounding in love and faithfulness, maintaining love to thousands, and forgiving wickedness, rebellion and sin.' (NIV)

After Moses broke the set of tablets of the ten commandments, the Israelites might have thought their relationship with God was over. They'd sinned too much; turned away from him one time too many. But that's not God's character. Instead, he welcomes the errant people back into his fold. Asking Moses to prepare new stone tablets, he renews his covenant with them.

In doing so, he names some of his attributes, those which never change. He is compassionate, a word in the Hebrew that connotes the womb. How lovely to think of God as a loving mother who does not forget the children birthed in her own body! (See Isaiah 49:15, which echoes this thought.)

And the Lord is gracious, showing grace to those who don't deserve it. He's slow to anger, not reaching boiling point when many humans would have exploded long before. Just think back over the readings thus far – God is certainly patient with the Israelites, just as he is with us.

He abounds in love and faithfulness, 'maintaining love to thousands' (v. 7). We say that God is 'love'. A way to understand the depth of this word is to witness the redeeming actions of God, seeing how he saves his people again and again. And, of course, he maintains his love to thousands of generations – to us – through the saving work of Jesus on the cross.

He forgives wickedness, rebellion and sin. Everyone living has fallen short of the glory of God. We've all sinned against him, and each other. But our gracious and compassionate God doesn't define us by our wrongdoing, but by his forgiveness. He extends the freedom of the cross to us, and we can extend it to others.

What a wonderful God we serve!

Lord, you show me what it means to love, and what it means to be gracious and compassionate. May I embrace your attributes today, living for and with you and sharing your love with others.

AMY BOUCHER PYE

The glory of the Lord

Then Moses set up the courtyard around the tabernacle and altar and put up the curtain at the entrance to the courtyard. And so Moses finished the work. Then the cloud covered the tent of meeting, and the glory of the Lord filled the tabernacle. (NIV)

We've seen plagues of hail and blood, lice and frogs. We've heard of Pharaoh's oppression and hard-heartedness, and Moses' repeated requests to let his people go. We've witnessed the miracles of the waves and wind as the Israelites left slavery behind. God has extended his covenant with his people, but they turned from him after a short time, to worship a man-made god of gold. Moses pleaded on their behalf, and God's relented. He has declared his attributes of love, compassion, grace, mercy and forgiveness. And in our final reading in Exodus together, we focus on God's presence with his people.

The Lord gives Moses many instructions on how they are to live, and as we see, 'Moses did everything just as the Lord commanded him' (v. 16). No ifs, ands or buts this time, saying he's not equipped or asking his brother to stand in for him. Rather, we see quiet obedience. The Lord responds by filling the newly constructed tabernacle – his physical home with his people – with his presence. His glory is so strong and holy that not even Moses can enter the tabernacle. And the cloud by day, and the fire in the cloud by night, remains on the tabernacle, reminding them that God is with them.

I hope from our fortnight together you will especially hold to this one central truth of the gospel: our loving God is with us. When we accept God's invitation to make his home with us, the indwelling of the Holy Spirit of Jesus guarantees we'll never again be alone. God will never leave us nor forsake us. Whatever storms may assail us, we can cling to the truth of this promise.

May you go forth in joy, loving and serving the saving God who created and formed us, he who will never leave us.

Lord, you loved the Israelites, leading them out of slavery and into a spacious place. Release me from whatever chains bind me, that I might love and serve you in constancy and peace.

AMY BOUCHER PYE

The treasure of scripture: Psalm 119

Michele D. Morrison writes:

'Draw near to God, and he'll draw near to you,' James wrote. As I visit my ten-month-old grandson, I am blessed with the sight of a child cuddling into his father and then relaxing as his dad holds him close. He knows the sound of his daddy's voice, the smell of his shaving lotion and the feel of his clothes. He knows he is safe and he is loved.

How do we, physical beings, draw near to our spiritual Father? God wants much more than our intellectual assent to the truths contained in scripture. He longs for us to draw near, and linger, and relax. He invites us to 'walk in the garden' with him. How?

Have you ever received a love letter? For most of us, they may be rare, but my husband Don and I fell in love through daily letters. We have them in a box, and it's fascinating now to see how our relationship deepened as we were honest and open with one another. But now I am describing something analytically, from a dispassionate distance. Forty-four years ago, every time I received a letter from Scotland, I ripped it open, read it through once, twice, 20 or 30 times, savouring every word, trying to pick up every nuance.

The Bible is God's love letter to us. When I was born again, I was so eager to read scripture, delighting in every word, rejoicing in God's presence. I drew nearer to him and revelled in his closeness more each day.

A couple of years ago, I attended the Cherish conference in Leeds and listened to Lisa Harper's teaching on Song of Songs. She opened up that book to me and confirmed my thinking that God chose, with deep care, to give us the image of Jesus as the bridegroom and the church as the bride of Christ. The concept of our relationship with the Almighty correlating to that of a husband and wife is shocking, but also deeply moving. The more mutual self-giving of husband and wife, the stronger love grows, and the same is true of our love for God. Draw near to God, and he'll draw near to you.

Over this fortnight, my prayer is that as we look at Psalm 119, we all fall deeper in love with the living Word through the written word.

Golden words

I will praise you with an upright heart as I learn your righteous laws. I will obey your decrees; do not utterly forsake me. (NIV)

Decrees are statements of authoritative truth. Learning and obeying God's decrees grounds us in the truth of who God is and what his will is, and has the power to change circumstances and change us. In Hebrew, the word for decree (*gazar*) means 'to divide, separate, destroy', and carries with it the idea that when God's decrees are spoken out, internalised and obeyed, the enemy's plans are thwarted.

Decrees establish foundations for our love for God and help release praise. 'Joyful are those who obey his laws and search for him with all their hearts' (v. 2, NLT).

Praise is powerful. Several years ago, God asked me to praise him for 30 minutes every day during Lent. This was a serious challenge: to praise – not give thanks, but praise – was difficult. I often praised along with David in Psalms: praising God for the world as he has decreed it: beautiful, unshakeable, his; praising him for his character: goodness, kindness, faithfulness, love; praising him for the gifts of Jesus and the Holy Spirit.

Just before Easter that year, I ended up in hospital. I was awoken in the night by a patient in the next room, in distress and being helped. As I lay awake, I decided to have my 30-minute praise time. It was 3.00 am, and as I praised God lifted me and gave me a foretaste of heaven. I lingered there not half an hour, but an hour and a half. It was as if the light of heaven shone in that room and I knew my Father's powerful presence.

Obeying God's decrees is not easy and we often fall short. But as we draw near to God and ask his help in praising, he takes us in his arms and loves us.

Oh God, you have decreed blessing on your people and you are faithful and powerful. Lord, I praise your name. Help me to immerse myself in your word and find you there.

MICHELE D. MORRISON

How do I love thee?

I have hidden your word in my heart that I might not sin against you. (NIV)

When I was a schoolgirl, we had to memorise some things by rote. It seemed not to matter whether or not you understood it, as long as you could repeat it word for word, be it a poem, a speech, historic dates and actions, or a song. We hid these things in our brains, and some of them are still retrievable in mine!

I am challenged by David's statement that he hid God's word in his heart. That implies more than learning by rote, because it involved his emotions as well as his mind. By hiding his word in our hearts, we connect our love with the love of God, and that transforms strict obedience out of duty into careful obedience out of love. Sometimes 'religion' can become rigid and loveless, lacking compassion and grace. It may be semantics, but I know believers who avoid the label 'religious', because of the rigid connotations that it can suggest. We've all known, or at least read about, fierce Christians who adhere absolutely to every dot of the law but who fail to adhere to love. In Jesus' day, many of these were called Pharisees.

'I meditate on your precepts and consider your ways' (v. 15). This takes time, but the reward is a closer relationship with the Father. Memorising scripture should be undertaken not so that we can quote it proudly, but so that we can mull it over as we drive, do the dishes or lie awake in the night, and allow it to change us. I don't think the version matters as long as it has captured the spirit of the verses. 'How do I love thee? Let me count the ways,' Elizabeth Barrett Browning wrote. Try it with God.

If I can memorise a little bite of scripture every day, at the end of a year I will have a larder filled with nourishment and life, to be chewed over during days both easy and challenging.

MICHELE D. MORRISON

Don't be a stranger

Open my eyes that I may see wonderful things in your law... My soul is consumed with longing for your laws at all times... Your statutes are my delight; they are my counsellors. (NIV)

Reading the Bible without the help of the Holy Spirit leaches the life out of the word. I used to think scripture was dry as dust, but after the life-changing night when I was filled with the Spirit, I could not get enough of my Bible. As soon as I got our two wee ones tucked up for the night, I sat for hours devouring my Bible. I met God at a new level, where he opened my eyes, inspired and changed me. His words became my counsellors. It was at a time when homesickness was my constant, gnawing companion, and I hear that same aching loneliness in these verses. 'I am a stranger' (v. 19).

We are never strangers to God. He knows us better than we know ourselves, and he delights to pull back the veil which shades the word and take us deeper into him.

The deep veins of golden advice and the heartbeat of God are revealed as we meditate on his word. In a prayer group, the leader invited us to sit with a short passage of scripture, explaining that after 20 minutes we would each share what the Lord said to us. What he said to me seemed so obvious that I was sure everyone would hear the same thing. I was amazed when he spoke different words of life to each individual.

Christian mindfulness is a new term for the ancient practice of contemplative prayer and meditation. Somehow, the church let this precious discipline slip and the benefits of quiet thought became associated with eastern religions. It's time we recognise and value the gift the Lord has given us. It is incredible to be invited to sit and share time and thoughts with the Almighty God and king of creation.

'Don't be a stranger,' we may say to a new neighbour or friend. Hear God saying it to you, today, as you enjoy his company in his word.

MICHELE D. MORRISON

A bank of consolation

My soul is weary with sorrow; strengthen me according to your word. (NIV)

I have been laid low in the dust – when untimely bereavement robbed me of my sister and a baby grandson. When these tragedies overtook me, there was a numbness and a sense of detached unreality that kept me in a routine and protected me from indulging the howling grief that might otherwise have controlled me. I hung in close to God, wearily clinging to him for strength.

I know no better way to deal with the disappointments and sorrows of life than to open oneself to God and invite the Holy Spirit to drip-feed scripture into one's deepest being. With my sister's death, I repeated Psalm 63 like a mantra: 'Because your love is better than life, my lips will glorify you.' Those words strengthened me through the dark hours of the night. With my baby grandson's death, Isaiah 61:2–3 encouraged me: God promises 'to comfort all who mourn, and provide for those who grieve in Zion – to bestow on them a crown of beauty instead of ashes, the oil of joy instead of mourning, and a garment of praise instead of a spirit of despair'.

Storing up God's word in our memory banks is wise. We never know what lies around the corner, and God's word is like a hotline into his own heart, confirming that he is with us in our sorrows as he is in our joys, weeping with us, holding us close, whether or not we understand what is going on.

Notice the movement of these few verses: the psalmist goes from being laid low in the dust to running in the path of God's commandments: from prostration to action. The word of God has the power to revive and restore.

Lord God, help me to build up a bank of rich words on which I can draw when things go wrong. Thank you that you never leave nor forsake any of us, Jesus.

MICHELE D. MORRISON

Freedom!

Turn my heart towards your statutes and not towards selfish gain. Turn my eyes away from worthless things… I will walk about in freedom, for I have sought out your precepts. (NIV)

People long to win the lottery, thinking riches will free them to choose the way they live. It's a deceit, though: winners often confess that the money made them miserable.

Our material world entangles us in the cords of consumerism. Internet shopping fuels desire and makes acquisition of worthless things easy. I live in a rambling house with barns packed with stuff. Instead of boxes of 'valuables' in my barn, I want to have a treasure chest of scripture in my heart, so that if I end my days in the fog of dementia, my spirit will be sustained by that treasure.

My ambition is to declutter before that time, and not leave my children with lots of worthless things. When my grandpa died at age 80, his worldly possessions were contained in one cardboard box. He travelled light.

The real treasure in life is freely available to all, and it is found in God's word. Meditating on his word enriches us as it takes us deeper into the mysteries of his loving being. Those riches can never be lost or stolen.

Jesus knew the scriptures. He not only quoted them, but he lived them, recognising that many Old Testament prophecies were about him. He loved his Father and spent hours, often entire nights, in prayerful communion with him. He loved God's precepts, and perhaps his power was derived in part from that love for God's decrees.

It takes time to learn scripture, so in this age when time is nibbled away by social media and television, we need to ask God to give us a desire to know his word, so that we prioritise that. When we understand God and who we are in him, we are free – free indeed!

Father, give us this day our daily bread, both that which we consume and that which we ingest spiritually.

MICHELE D. MORRISON

Relief in the darkness

Your decrees have been the theme of my songs wherever I have lived. I reflect at night on who you are, O Lord; therefore, I obey your instructions. (NLT)

I was listening to a Chris Tomlin CD, and suddenly the song 'Our God' started playing. The lines came to life, and I understood the power of declaring God's control over one or two situations close to my heart, so I sang with faith and fervour and I am believing for a change in circumstances. Christian music can be powerful and move the soul into heaven's realms. It can raise expectations of our God, who is always good. It can root us in his promises and his character.

It's important to engage with music carefully, because songs can become 'ear worms'; as they echo through our minds, they have power to transform our thinking. That is great when we listen to music that is closely based on scripture and the truths of God. I see a real correlation between music and night-time reflections, as I often waken with a song in my head. Even asleep, I believe we can be reflecting on who God is. There are many wonderful praise songs based on scripture.

Darkness isn't only nocturnal. Many of us suffer in a shadowy world of depression. Can scripture shine light into the dark night of the soul? After World War II, many veterans suffering PTSD were hospitalised, and as community groups entertained with hymns and music, improvements in the patients were noted. That was the birth of modern music therapy, a recognised therapy used in conjunction with other therapies to treat depression and anxiety.

I don't want to trivialise clinical depression with a glib assertion that scriptural songs will drive it away. When we are sick, we need doctors. But soaking in the truths expressed in, say, Hillsong's 'What a beautiful name it is', may hasten the dawn.

Father, I thank you for the gift of music and the technology we have today, enabling us to worship in our own living rooms, alone or with others who know and love your name.

MICHELE D. MORRISON

Engaging the heart

With all my heart I want your blessings. Be merciful as you promised. I pondered the direction of my life, and I turned to follow your laws. (NLT)

Engage the heart. Crave the presence of the Lord. Studying scripture reveals to the psalmist that the way he is living his life is not in line with God's laws. He acknowledges that his suffering was good because it drove, or drew, him to God, helping him regain a proper perspective on what is really of value.

The psalmist proclaims that God is good and that what he does is good. This is a solid foundation on which to build a successful life. Knowing deep down in my soul that God is good, and trusting that he is with me in all that happens to me, frees me to step into the unknown future.

Walking in faith does not give us a full picture of the path ahead. God reveals the way one step at a time. I love the scene in *Indiana Jones and the Last Crusade* (1989), where Indiana steps off a cliff into an apparent chasm; it's only as he steps out in faith that the bridge rises up to meet him. The first step demands a lot of courage.

Someone close to me is considering the path of her life right now. She longs for God to teach her good judgement and knowledge, just as the psalmist craves. As she looks into scripture, the light within her is growing stronger and her strength to step out is encouraged. The waiting is hard, but the Lord is faithful.

There are no shortcuts in the journey of eternal life with God. The road may be rutted and winding, but trusting that God walks with us every step of the way gives us courage to walk beyond the map. 'Eating' the word and letting it digest in your soul has power to transform your thinking and inspire your courage.

Do you want God's blessings with all your heart? Remember his promises and step out. And may the road rise up to meet you.

MICHELE D. MORRISON

Persevering hope

My soul faints with longing for your salvation, but I have put my hope in your word. My eyes fail, looking for your promise; I say, 'When will you comfort me?' (NIV)

Stephen was diagnosed with motor neurone disease. As the disease progressed, his familiar walk became a painful stagger, then he moved into a wheelchair and finally a motorised buggy. Every Sunday morning, he could be seen propelling himself down the hill to church, his loving, faithful wife Mary beside him.

As the disease took its terrible toll, he kept his eyes fixed on the Lord. As I write, he passed into the Lord's presence two days ago. The one muscle that hadn't atrophied was his smile: an hour before he died, his pregnant daughter lovingly put his hand on her bump and he smiled to feel the baby moving within.

I can't think of a better example of a saint living in faith, hoping and trusting in the Lord until the end, surrounded by a loving wife and family, doing the same. Now his comfort has come.

'O God, you are my God; I earnestly search for you. My soul thirsts for you; my whole body longs for you in this parched and weary land where there is no water' (Psalm 63:1, NLT).

'How long must I wait?' the psalmist asks. How long? How do we wait in hope when things seem bleak? The only way I know of is by focusing on God. Focusing on circumstances only takes us down into darker valleys. Focusing on God, the lover of our souls, inspires us to take heart and persevere in hope. Imbibing the promises of God is the way to live life to the full, whatever limitations constrict us.

The best and truest way to focus on God is to gaze at him as revealed in scripture. Studying his attributes and the character and life of Jesus develops our spiritual hunger, which is only satisfied by God's magnificent presence.

The more we taste and see that the Lord is good, the more every fibre of our beings is refreshed.

MICHELE D. MORRISON

Heavenly perspective

Your word, Lord, is eternal; it stands firm in the heavens. Your faithfulness continues through all generations; you established the earth, and it endures. (NIV)

Occasionally, I find myself in one of those quirky shops that has an eclectic mix of merchandise, including various wall decorations inscribed with worldly wisdom. 'You are what you eat.' 'What goes around, comes around.' 'Everything happens for a reason.' 'Stop watering the weeds in your life and start watering the flowers.'

Some of these clever sayings may have merit; many of them are mere platitudes. God's sayings, on the other hand, stand like a giant redwood tree, huge trunk stretching to the skies, held firm by many sturdy roots. As evocative a picture as that is to a California girl, it doesn't begin to touch the truth of the reliability of God's word. Here, the psalmist describes it as eternal, standing firm in the heavens.

At a conference, I saw a picture taken by Voyager I as it left the solar system in 1990, 14 years after it was launched from earth. The famous picture, which Karl Sagan called the 'pale blue dot', shows streams of varying colours, resembling shafts of light, and in one of them, a pale blue dot – the earth – is easily distinguished. We can only imagine the vastness of the 'heavens', the universe: what, indeed, is humanity when seen against such an enormous canvas? And yet, humanity was worth dying for, Jesus thought. Not just humanity, but you. 'For God so loved the world that he gave his one and only Son, that whoever believes in him shall not perish but have eternal life' (John 3:16).

'The wicked are waiting to destroy me, but I will ponder your statutes' (v. 95). In other words, I will sit down at a table with you, absorbed by your beauty and nourished by you, and though my enemies surround me, I am blissfully unaware because I am so in love with you.

I love you, Lord. In your presence I find life itself; I find strength and my song. My enemies pale to insignificance in the radiance of your glorious presence. I love you, Lord.

MICHELE D. MORRISON

Developing your sweet tooth

How sweet are your words to my taste, sweeter than honey to my mouth! I gain understanding from your precepts; therefore I hate every wrong path. (NIV)

Sugar is addictive. A sweet tooth leads to no tooth. Too much sugar results in obesity and disease. But a taste for the sweetness of the word of God leads to life in all its fullness. As we chew over the word of God, it releases wisdom and understanding, which build up our souls and enrich our spirits.

Spending time in God's word, though, doesn't just enrich our own lives; it transforms our actions so that we become a blessing to the world in which we live. 'Your word is a lamp for my feet, a light on my path' (v. 105). When my actions spring from my interaction with the Lord, the world's reaction is to recognise the glory of God.

Jesus said that he only did what his Father did, and in Jesus God was glorified. The closer we are to the Lord, the more powerful our evangelistic footprint will become – not through persuasive words but through inspirational lives.

Not only does the word of God help us to recognise the tempting paths that lead to destruction for what they are, but it also illuminates the next step on the path God calls us to walk.

God's law is the joy of the psalmist's heart and his inheritance. As I wrote earlier, when I was born again, I couldn't get enough of God's word, which had suddenly come alive to me. Nearly 40 years on, I still love my Bible and take it wherever I go. Recently, my husband and I undertook a pilgrimage, and although I ditched make-up and hair sprays because of the weight in my backpack, I never considered leaving behind my pocket Bible.

His word is my guide, a touchstone to eternity and to his loving presence. I am so blessed to have so many Bible editions.

Lord, I love your word. I love your written word, and I love your living Word, Jesus Christ, my Saviour. Forever I will sing your praises and give you thanks for the fullness of life you've gifted to me.

MICHELE D. MORRISON

Do something, Lord!

It is time for you to act, Lord; your law is being broken. (NIV)

We usually watch the news after dinner, but every so often we take a sabbatical from it. We hear the dire stories on the radio; the headlines appear on the Twitter feed and embed themselves in my Facebook feed. Enough!

Politicians wrangle and squirm; some are deceitful, and some are honest. There are nations in upheaval, in pain and soaked in blood. The innocent languish in dirty jails. Even in the church, there are men and women of deceit and evil intent. The environment is being trashed. When we watch the news, we groan from the deepest parts of ourselves: it is time for you to act, Lord!

This section of Psalm 119 reveals a heart depending on the Lord to make righteous changes to the world's systems and people. When the writer feels at his weakest, he appeals to the Lord for salvation. He continually cites scripture as the source of strength and righteousness.

We Christians are doubly blessed. Not only do we have the written word, but we also have the living Word and the Holy Spirit residing in us. If the psalmist could rely on God through his word, how much more should we be able to lean close to God and find our source of strength and salvation in him!

We have a God of justice and mercy. When was the last time you were on your knees before him, surrendering all your deepest desires and wishes to his will, and petitioning him for the sake of others, for the sake of the world? I do it too rarely. He is waiting to intervene, to defend and uphold and bring about change. The church is the people of the word, and we have access to the source of unlimited power. Let's lean close, look up and cry out.

Lord, hear us as we cry out for our wounded, broken world – your wounded, broken world. Father, pour out your Spirit, fill us and embolden us to turn things round. In your name.

MICHELE D. MORRISON

Hidden truths

The unfolding of your words gives light; it gives understanding to the simple. (NIV)

Are you old enough to remember those Magic Eye pictures with the images cleverly concealed within their busy patterns? My Uncle Bill was so delighted with the hidden depths of such pictures that he had one or two on his wall and enjoyed watching visitors struggle to discern what was hidden within the swirling colours and twisting shapes. Relax the eyes, was his advice, and imagine focusing your gaze just beyond what you can see. I remember feeling pressured to see the hidden image, feeling foolish until suddenly it emerged. Magic – hiding in plain sight!

God gives us his word, which has power and meaning when we read it as normal. But when we linger over it, allowing it to speak to our deepest being… when we unfold it… we gain wisdom and understanding. Such insight fills us with awe and wonder and leads us into praise and worship.

'The teaching of your word gives light' (v. 130, NLT). Indeed, a good teacher can enhance our understanding through giving us historical insights and facts. Meditating on the word, chewing it over alone with God, makes the message personal to our present circumstance and reveals God within those circumstances.

The psalmist declares that he is so eager to understand God, he pants with expectation and longing. Dogs pant when they have been running hard, and cats pant when they are in pain. When events overwhelm me, I pant (metaphorically) for God's word. How often his word has given me comfort and strength when facing all kinds of trials!

In God's word, there are depths to be plumbed. As we linger with the Bible, God is freed to reveal himself, and us, at deeper levels. Let the Son of God enfold you.

'Trust in God,' Jesus said, 'and trust also in me. There is more than enough room in my Father's home' (John 14:1–2). Lord, open my eyes to see my true identity, and yours, within your precious living word.

MICHELE D. MORRISON

Absolute truth! Forever!

All your words are true; all your righteous laws are eternal. (NIV)

Absolute truth forever: such is the written word of God. Such is the 'Word [who] became flesh and dwelt among us' (John 1:14, ESV), Jesus Christ.

These verses reveal the anxious thoughts of one overcome by troubles, crying out to the Lord for help, again and again. The condition for receiving help, as the psalmist understands it, is obedience to the word. It's not that help is withheld unless you obey the law; it's that help is released when you cry out to the God you love.

This is exactly what Jesus taught: 'If you love me, keep my commands. And I will ask the Father, and he will give you another advocate to help you and be with you forever – the Spirit of truth' (John 14:15–17).

Psalm 119:136 says, 'Streams of tears flow from my eyes, for your law is not obeyed.' It breaks our hearts when someone we love does not have a right relationship with Jesus. In the same way, the psalmist loves the Lord, hangs on his every word, and longs for others to enjoy God.

Love for God, and the reliability and truth of his word: this precept should underpin all our evangelism. Love for Jesus and further revelations of God's character grow as we engage with his word. Absolute truths are so antithetical to the current worldview: the world is full of fake news, smoke and mirrors, lies presented as truths.

Only the word of God is true. Only Jesus is the way, the truth and the life.

Almighty heavenly Father God, thank you that every word you have spoken is true and that the living Word, Jesus, is the living truth.

MICHELE D. MORRISON

Bringing peace, joy and singing

Great peace have those who love your law, and nothing can make them stumble. I wait for your salvation, Lord, and I follow your commands. (NIV)

There is a sedate rhythm to this long psalm, with a chorus of joy winding through the verses extolling the virtues of God's law. Jesus came not to abolish the law but to fulfil it. He is the word made flesh and in him is life in all its fullness, joy without end, and peace beyond our understanding. God's written word is absolutely honest and reveals his unconditionally loving heart. Why would we not want to lose ourselves in the Bible, the greatest of all love letters? There is an explosion of joy as this great psalm comes to an end.

My fourth-grade teacher, Mrs Costuma, taught us to tie every piece of writing up with a red ribbon: 'Conclude with what you stated at the beginning.' The psalmist claims in verse 1: 'Joyful are people of integrity.' And now, he ends with a crescendo of joy: 'I rejoice in your word like one who discovers a great treasure' (v. 162); 'I will praise you seven times a day' (v. 164); 'let praise flow from my lips' (v. 171); 'let my tongue sing about your word' (v. 172); 'let me live so I can praise you' (v. 175).

Great peace is promised to those who love God. At one of the most traumatic times of my life, when I had to move my dear mother into a residential facility, I walked a dark road. By God's grace, during those turbulent days, I clung to the Lord, and he filled me with great peace and strength. He lit the path ahead and he comforted me. His peace released me to sing his praises. His peace released joy. As I drove in tears from my childhood home to the new residence, I heard him whisper: 'In every teardrop there is a rainbow.' Yes, he gave me peace, hope and quiet joy.

Peace leads to singing: may my tongue sing of the treasure chest that is your word, for all your commands are righteous. May my lips overflow with praise.

MICHELE D. MORRISON

Christian conduct: 1 Corinthians

Rachel Turner writes:

If I was given a time machine, I definitely would go back and visit the early church. While the early church had some wonderful holy moments, it was fantastically messy as well. People of different ethnicities and religions were all discovering together a whole new way of life with a whole new theology of how to live, pray and be a community.

It did not always go smoothly.

That's why I love 1 Corinthians. This church was started by Paul and his friends in Corinth in Greece. For a few years, he worked as a tent-maker and shared about Jesus with the Jews. When the Jewish authorities became abusive, he started talking about Jesus to the Gentiles too. Eventually, people of many backgrounds began to become Christians and gather together, each bringing their diverse religious experiences to bear on their new learnings about Jesus. Paul left to continue his journeys, and the church in Corinth grew as they tried to figure out how to live according to what Paul had taught them about Jesus.

It appears they wrote him a follow-up letter, asking him questions about things like marriage and sex, and eating food sacrificed to idols. But Paul had other reports, from people whom he trusted, that gave him a fuller picture of what was happening in the church. While they were genuinely trying to follow Christ, they also were getting drunk at Communion and insulting each other, talking over each other while praying during worship, divided about issues of ethnicity and leadership, and some members were even involved in prostitution and incest.

Yep, the early church was not dull.

So Paul wrote a letter back to them, to address their questions and to challenge them on all the other stuff he had heard about too. He wrote back to them specifically, but also addressed the wider church, knowing that what he was writing would encourage more than just the church in Corinth. A significant portion of it talks about Christian conduct, not surprisingly. For the next couple of weeks, we will be looking at the wisdom with which Paul counselled these early church Christians, and in so doing be encouraged ourselves.

See our faults through the lens of truth

I thank God because in Christ you have been made rich in every way, in all your speaking and in all your knowledge. (NCV)

I remember when I first started leading people, I was trained in how to give feedback to my team. My boss called it a 'praise sandwich': start off and end with genuine praise, and sandwich the constructive or correctional 'bad' news in the middle to help the negative input be seen within the wider positive context.

Paul's letter to the Corinthians is full of corrections and opinions. But Paul doesn't start off with: 'Okay church, what's with the rumours I hear, and your last letter to me? (*sigh*) Come on! You are *killing* me here. What are you *thinking*?' No, he starts off simply with love, with joy, with gratefulness for their existence and with an affirmation of the truth.

Paul reassures the Corinthians that God the Father has given them grace and love through Jesus. He has given them gifts, knowledge and the truth to hold on to. God has promised to strengthen them, and enables them to be blameless before the coming King because of his grace and love. He assures them that he prays for them and acknowledges them as 'called to be holy' and a part of the beauty of the wider church. He builds them up. Even knowing what he will say next, he wants them to hear it knowing this assurance first.

That's quite a start.

There are so many times in my life when I see all my imperfections, all my failures, all the bits where I have got it wrong, and I forget that God sees me first as a loved child of his, covered in his grace and love, filled with his gifts and knowledge, and locked into Jesus' holiness and companionship. It is only through that lens of truth that I begin the journey of aligning my conduct to God's character.

God, thank you for giving your gifts, knowledge, love and grace to me, even though I am an imperfect person. Please show me where in my life I have forgotten that, so I can welcome you in.

RACHEL TURNER

Persevere through brain fog

(Yes, I also baptised the household of Stephanas; beyond that, I don't remember if I baptised anyone else.) (NIV)

I don't know about you, but in my life I have encountered seasons of 'brain fog'. You know how it goes, I'm sure. You head purposefully into a room, and then have no idea why you went in. You can't complete a sentence because all your words run away from you, so you're just left open-mouthed searching for the rest of your thought, but it's just gone. You search for five minutes for the phone that you are currently talking on.

For us women, whether it's 'baby brain', a monthly blip or the chaos that happens during menopause, there can be moments where our memory fails us. I remember when clinical menopause hit me like a ton of bricks after a hysterectomy. I was worried that I would be lost in the fog forever. And I was worried how that would impact on my ability to serve God.

I love this passage in 1 Corinthians. Paul is talking about important problems like unity and jealousy within the church, but in the middle of his argument, he admits to the limits of his memory. He openly and unashamedly says, 'I only baptised these two guys. Oh yeah, and that one family. I can't remember if I baptised anyone else' (my very loose paraphrase). Anyway, back to my argument… It makes me smile because in this moment of honesty, Paul shows me how to persevere in the midst of brain fog. That it is okay for my brain not to remember perfectly all the time. Because God is calling me to speak, to minister, to argue and to encourage. And if my brain fogs for a bit, fine, I'll do my best, acknowledge it with no embarrassment and get back to speaking God's words to others.

Take a moment to tell God how you feel when brain fog happens to you, and ask him to pour his grace, peace and confidence into you so you can continue to do what he is asking you to do with power and purpose.

RACHEL TURNER

Rest on God's power

My teaching and preaching were not with words of human wisdom that persuade people but with proof of the power that the Spirit gives. This was so that your faith would be in God's power and not in human wisdom. (NCV)

Almost every time I speak in front of people, I get nervous. If I let my mind wander, I become overwhelmed with the responsibility of it all: the need to be funny, clear, wise and useful. I think, 'If I can just say everything right, I may be able to serve God well today.' And then I go and read some of Paul. Paul was super qualified, a scholar under the famous teacher Gamaliel. Paul knew his stuff and knew how to argue. And yet he openly admitted that he was weak and afraid when he was teaching, and that he wasn't brilliant at persuading people.

Instead, he says, it was his demonstration of God's power that did the persuading.

I am so grateful he said this, because if Paul's success was because he was a once-in-a-millennium kind of guy, then I could write him off as a one off super apostle whom God raised up to change the world, and very different from me. But if Paul was just a normal guy, a bit hot-headed, who still struggled with insecurity and self-doubt, and yet God worked through him anyway, well then, God can work through me too!

God's power isn't dependent on anyone. He can move when he wants and how he wants, and yet we get to be alongside him in his great work. He faithfully completes what he sets out to do, and we can follow him, partnering with him when he invites us, and doing what he says,

We will never be so good that we feel worthy of what God calls us to. That's okay. He just wants us alongside him, imperfect as we are.

Thank you, Lord, for loving me so much that you invite me to do your work alongside you.

RACHEL TURNER

Come alongside others

I planted the seed, Apollos watered it, but God has been making it grow. (NIV)

Do you remember the people who helped shape your faith? I can try to list mine, but the list soon becomes too long to write. One professor I had in university invested huge amounts of time in me and challenged me deeply about how I acted and thought. A preacher gave one sermon that rocked my world and became a foundation for my life, but I never had a conversation with him. One elderly person at my church was open about how God walked with him as he was dying and provided the basis for how I personally dealt with cancer. I can list so many people who shaped me and encouraged me in my faith, and I'm sure you can too.

Paul encourages the Corinthians not to follow one person exclusively, but rather to see that God is growing them through the different influences of many. It makes me think about how significant we all are in the lives of others and how they may list us in their stories of faith.

I want to be bold in coming alongside people for a season, knowing that my little bit contributes to God's great plans for their growth. I want to look out for those whom God has placed in my path, ready to play my part.

I also want to let go of fears and worries for those no longer in my sphere of influence, trusting that God is bringing others into their lives who will continue the work he has started. Whether it is our children, friends or people we have mentored or helped, God is growing them, and bringing others in to plant and water what he is doing.

I have faith for that.

God, I am ready and willing to plant or water what you are doing in the lives of those around me. Thank you that I can trust you to provide others to come alongside those I love, to help them grow in you.

RACHEL TURNER

Act for the audience of one

He will bring to light what is hidden in darkness and will expose the motives of the heart. At that time each will receive their praise from God. (NIV)

In the steaming hot school hall, all I could see was the top of my kid's ginger head, weaving side-to-side at the back of the stage. Up front were 80 kids holding recorders, waiting to perform, and hundreds of parents and carers bracing ourselves for the pain of a recorder recital. My boy's face lit up in a smile as he crouched down between the heads of two older girls to find me in the crowd. Throughout the next four songs, he played his heart out, his eyes flicking back to me every few seconds to watch my reaction. There were hundreds of people in the room, but he was playing for an audience of one.

In this passage, Paul is trying to get the Corinthian church to stop fighting about which leader is better, and who has greater status because of who they follow. As he does this, he explains that each one of us, including himself, is simply a servant of Christ, trying to be faithful to what we are asked to do, solely focused on pleasing God; the one who is the ultimate judge, who sees and knows all. We are playing for an audience of one.

In the daily grind of life, in all our roles in our families, communities or work, it can be so easy to judge ourselves by what others see, or even by the standards we hold ourselves to. But Paul encourages us to ignore not only the judgement of others, but also of ourselves. There is only one judge to whom our eyes should constantly flick as we make our choices each day: the one being who sees the depths of our hearts, and loves us anyway, cheering us on as our lives play a song of imperfect praise to him.

God, I place my life before you with an open heart. Search my heart, bring light where it is needed, and help me hear your fatherly voice as you guide, comfort, challenge and encourage me.

RACHEL TURNER

Embrace the responsibility of freedom

'I have the right to do anything,' you say – but not everything is beneficial. 'I have the right to do anything' – but I will not be mastered by anything. (NIV)

So, let's talk about incest. Ha! I bet you didn't wake up today thinking, 'You know what I want to read about in my Bible today? Really messed up family life – that will do my heart good!' I am so sorry. Paul talks about all sorts of things in his letters – and so we must wade in too.

Evidently, in the church in Corinth, there was a guy who decided that he was going to have a relationship with his dad's wife. And from what we can tell from Paul's letter, it appears that the church responded by saying something like, 'Well Jesus frees us from the law, so we can do whatever we want! Woohoo!' Paul is horrified and spends several chapters responding to this errant belief. And we, as modern Christians, can surely shake our heads smugly at the waywardness of the early church.

Except a niggling thought keeps at me. Is what they were saying so far from how I behave sometimes? No, not incest, but how often do I let my sin slide because of my assurance that God will forgive me? How often do I let my words speak unwisely about a colleague or friend, and then excuse it as simply 'processing' an experience? And when I let my heart dwell on anger or self-pity, do I even register it as sinful?

I am struck by how oblivious the Corinthians were. They thought they were truly living in the freedom of Christ, yet were sitting in sin. Like the Corinthians, I sometimes need to be reminded that Jesus' grace was to reconcile us to God, not so we could live as we desire, but so we can live as he desires.

Father God, thank you for your grace, and for the freedom in Jesus you gave me. I want to live as you want me to live. Be my guide in discovering what true freedom in Christ is meant to be.

RACHEL TURNER

Sacrifice for the weak

But be careful that your freedom does not cause those who are weak in faith to fall into sin. (NCV)

Life in Corinth included a huge variety of other gods being worshipped. Whether it was Zeus, Dionysus, Artemis, Aphrodite or Apollo, if people wanted something, they could sacrifice meat or other items to a god for it. Any meat that the priests didn't eat would be sold cheaply in the local market. The debate began to rage among the new church. Was eating meat that had been sacrificed to idols a sin or not?

Paul had an interesting answer: what is most useful to the people around you?

We all understand this when it comes to drinking alcohol around a recovering alcoholic. We know that drinking around them may tempt them to drink, and so we choose to sacrifice our freedoms to support their continued sobriety: not to serve alcohol around them, or to meet in locations without a bar.

Paul is saying we should do nothing that will play on others' weaknesses and tempt them to sin. I'm struck, though, with how vulnerable we must be with each other to even know what those weaknesses are. Am I willing to share with my friends what temptations I am currently struggling with? Am I bold enough to say, 'Actually, I'm not up for that movie. Romcoms really suck me into not good places in my head' or, 'I think I get way too judgemental when we talk about work in this way; can we keep it positive, so my heart doesn't default to bitter?'

When we can be honest with what troubles or tempts us, then so can our friends. And when they do, we can be right there to support them. What if we could be the community of believers who genuinely strengthen each other by covering each other's weaknesses? All it takes is a bit of boldness and honesty.

Take some time to process with God where your weaknesses lie. What traps of sin do you tend to fall into that your friends could help you with?

RACHEL TURNER

Dealing with temptation

No temptation has overtaken you except what is common to [humankind]. And God is faithful; he will not let you be tempted beyond what you can bear. But when you are tempted, he will also provide a way out so that you can endure it. (NIV)

Have you ever seen those videos of self-control tests they do with children? They bring five-year-olds into a room one at a time and sit them at a table with an enormous marshmallow on it. They tell the child that in a moment, they will be popping out for a bit and will return. They tell the child that they can eat the marshmallow now or wait until the researcher returns. If they wait, they will receive an additional marshmallow. The researcher then leaves the room, and we get to watch a small person agonisingly resist the temptation to eat that marshmallow straightaway. The children fidget and sing, close their eyes, smell the marshmallow, talk to themselves, all in a desperate attempt to resist temptation.

The choices we make are so linked to what is internally pulling on us. Life can seem full of temptations. Temptations to compromise, temptations to hate or to cheat, to envy or to boast. Temptations to flirt or to let our hearts and minds dwell on thoughts that damage our connection with others. The temptations come often. Our response can be like the children's – a desperate avoidance and distraction. But that doesn't appear to be the biblical way to avoid sin. Jesus faced his temptations head-on with defiance and scripture (Matthew 4). Paul says that when temptation comes, God is faithful to provide a way out.

What if the way to deal with temptation is to engage with God, rather than hide? What if, instead of asking God to take the temptation away, we say, 'Okay God, this thing is pulling on me really hard. What is the way out? Lead me to the other side. I'm ready.'

Have a talk with God about what temptations to sin keep pulling on you. Ask him for the strategy of how to walk through it with him until you find the way out.

RACHEL TURNER

Use our gifts

All these are the work of one and the same Spirit, and he distributes them to each one, just as he determines. (NIV)

Our family has recently discovered cooperative games.

Cooperative games are board games with a twist. Rather than one player winning and the rest losing, a cooperative game puts all players on one team, and gives them a challenge. All players win and lose together. Usually, each player is given a role – a job within the team to fulfil. Each role comes with strengths and weaknesses, special skills or powers that only they can use. The challenge is to use each person's strengths and weaknesses and to try to conquer the task together.

It makes me reflect on how rare that experience is in normal Christian life. Paul assures us that each one of us is given gifts from God: skills and wisdom, aspects of God's heart and character. We are each given our individual gifts – not to give us an advantage over others, but so that we can join together, each bringing our gifts, in order to impact the world for God.

Whenever my family plays a cooperative game, we often take a while to get going. We read the rules and take ages to try to understand how each of our roles work, but often it still doesn't quite make sense. Then we play and, suddenly, the roles fall into place and we understand how it all works. So often, we as Christians waste so much time on the sidelines, holding ourselves back until we figure out our gifts and how they work. But they aren't meant to be understood in isolation. Sometimes we can only understand how our gifts work when we are finally using them, side-by-side with others, for the common good.

What is stirring your heart right now? Where do you want to serve? Be bold to start getting involved, trusting that God will give you the necessary gifts and a role to play.

RACHEL TURNER

Delight in the whole body

If the whole body were an eye, where would the sense of hearing be? If the whole body were an ear, where would the sense of smell be? (NIV)

Burned in my memory is the first time I visited a traditional high church service: the smell of the incense and the glow of the candles; the rustling of the congregation as they stood and knelt and sat down again; the peaceful silence and the beauty of the choir. It was so different from the church that I regularly attended, and yet I encountered the same God, and experienced him in a new way there.

I travel a lot for my work and have the privilege of meeting with people from many different denominations and doctrines. Every single time, I encounter some new aspect of God's heart, and am challenged in a fresh way. I am in awe at how such a range of people, worshipping God in such distinct and vibrant ways, all represent the God I love and serve.

As I read this passage, I notice how Paul is encouraging us as individuals to see ourselves as an essential part of the body – not so that we all become the same, but that in our differences we form a strong and unified whole; that in our differences, we may be effective in representing the heart and body of Jesus.

There is so much we can learn from each other's skills and life experiences. If we are an eye, and only share with other eyes, what will we miss out on? How often have you visited another church, just to experience God in a different way? How often do we laugh and talk with people called to different roles within the church? We are called to be a part of the body. Why not enjoy it all?

God, open my mind to see you within all Christians around me. Guide me to places where I can see something new about you. Thank you for welcoming me as part of this beautiful body.

RACHEL TURNER

Be willing to need others

The eye cannot say to the hand, 'I don't need you!' And the head cannot say to the feet, 'I don't need you!' (NIV)

I'm going to let you in on a secret: I quit my high school volleyball team because my coach made the perfectly reasonable decision to train some other people for the position that I played. My little ego couldn't handle it. I was incensed. I was hurt. In my deepest fear of all fears, I thought that she didn't need me. And so, I quit. Looking back, I roll my eyes at myself and think, 'Maybe I need some major prayer ministry to root out what that was all about.' The reality is that there is something in all of us that needs to be needed. There is something about belonging that is connected to other people needing us.

The problem is that sometimes in our church community, we see other people and we think, 'I value you, I'm glad you are here, but I don't *need* you.' Sometimes we think that about the children in our church, or the homeless fringe attendees on a Sunday evening. We live happily in our zone of the body of Christ and cheerfully encourage the others from afar.

But Paul says here that we can't do that. We do need each other. For us, and for them.

If we truly are to have 'no division in the body', we need to go on an exploration of connection. There was one elderly group of friends I knew who faithfully attended the contemporary evening service, because they thought all the 20s and 30s needed some grandparents to love them, and because they needed the fresh vitality of some passionate, goofy young Christians around them. So many lives were changed because of their choice.

The body of Christ is designed to flourish when we need each other. Are we ready for that?

God, break down the walls of my heart that keep me disconnected from others. Lead me to those that I need in my life, and to those that need me.

RACHEL TURNER

Love well

Love is patient, love is kind. It does not envy, it does not boast, it is not proud. (NIV)

One of the first sermons I ever remember hearing was on this passage. I remember the preacher repeating, 'Love is not an emotion. It is an action. You don't need to feel loving to choose to act lovingly.' He essentially told us to 'fake it till you make it' when it came to love. I tried. Boy, did I try! Oh, the debates I had with myself over 'What is the loving thing to do in this situation?'

This chapter kept pulling me back, though. Paul says here that all the supernatural gifts and all the super-spiritual actions are nothing without love. What if we are called not just to *act* lovingly, but genuinely to cultivate our hearts so that we *feel* love to those around us.

I don't think God just *acts* lovingly towards us. I believe that he loves us. When Jesus told us to love our enemies, I don't think he meant, 'Grit your teeth and figure out what acting lovingly in this situation means.' I think he meant for us to come close to his heart, be transformed by his love, peace and compassion, and genuinely love our enemies.

When Paul here describes love, I believe it is a description of what the love of God looks like when it flows from him, and when his love flows from us. It isn't a checklist of behaviours to wrestle with achieving. It's a mirror to our hearts, to ask ourselves, 'Am I genuinely full of God's love?'

God isn't calling us to force ourselves to be nice. He is asking us to say, 'Okay God, I want to love this person like you do. Show me what needs to change in my heart and mind to love her well.'

God, I want to love like you do. Help me see others through your eyes. Go through my heart and mind with me, God, and clear out what stops me from loving people well.

RACHEL TURNER

Stand firm

Always give yourselves fully to the work of the Lord, because you know that your labour in the Lord is not in vain. (NIV)

I once did a study on prisoners of war. I was fascinated with how individuals and groups persevered within such extreme environments. I was shocked when I discovered that one of the most effective techniques the guards employed to wear down the hope, morale and emotional endurance of the prisoners was pointless labour. Prisoners would tell stories of when they were pushed hard to dig a hole, and then were driven just as hard to fill it up again. Day after day, they were required to pour out their energy for nothing. And it broke many of them.

So many times in my life, I have felt like I have been pouring myself out for what seems like nothing. Whether it's the endless maintenance of the house, or keeping the email inbox from drowning me, or the monotony of sleepless baby nights, there are times when we all can begin to question, 'What am I pouring myself out for?'

Paul assures us of one thing: that when we give ourselves fully to the work of the Lord, we can be confident that it is always effective and worthwhile. And what is the work of the Lord? Amazingly, it is the stuff of life. None of our days is ever pointless or in vain, because in the ordinariness of life, we are doing the work of the Lord. Every time we are patient and kind with a difficult child, or a loved one with dementia, he promises it is not in vain. Every time we pause with compassion for someone who is struggling, we release his healing love. Every time we lead our work teams well, or pioneer with integrity, or do an ordinary day's work with the guidance of God, he is accomplishing his plans.

God, thank you for your faithfulness to work all things together for good. I give you my days, the extraordinary ones and the boring ones. Help me to give myself fully to your work each day.

RACHEL TURNER

I am what I am

But God's grace has made me what I am, and his grace to me was not wasted. (NCV)

Every time I read through 1 Corinthians, I stop at this little section, and read it over and over. Paul's life has been a rollercoaster journey, from privileged Roman citizen to disciple of a famous teacher, to fierce and proud persecutor of Christians, to a broken-down nobody and transformed follower of Jesus, to hidden years that we know nothing about, to a sharer of the gospel and challenger of apostles, to his missionary journeys, to shipwrecks and beatings, to amazing experiences of God's power… the story is long and complex.

In the middle of this letter, he says simply, 'All the other apostles are greater than I am. I am not even good enough to be called an apostle, because I persecuted the church of God. But God's grace has made me what I am, and his grace to me was not wasted' (vv. 9–10).

We are all on complicated, winding journeys with God. Our lives may have taken brutal disappointments or radical reformations. We may have walked away totally from him, or gone numb or silent, or our path may have been slow and steady with God. Each one of us has a unique story to tell, but we all can say with confidence that 'God's grace has made me what I am, and his grace to me was not wasted'.

Your journey is a worthy one. Your story is a powerful one. Whatever you have walked through to get to this moment, God has promised to turn it for good. Paul's early history was marked by opposition to God, which caused much suffering to others, and yet God used him mightily.

As you continue your journey with God, may he continue to encourage you and challenge you, as you align yourself each day with his word, and let his love strengthen you.

Take a moment to jot down on a piece of paper the ups and downs of your faith journey with God, and talk with Jesus about your feelings about them.

RACHEL TURNER

The grace of God: Jonah

Diana Archer writes:

'Have you heard the tale of Jonah and the whale?'

It could well be that a children's song is reverberating in your head at this very moment. It was certainly one of my kids' favourites. The tale of Jonah is a gift to children: it's vivid, memorable and dramatic. Pop-up Bible books, pictures to colour in, papier-mâché fish – Jonah and his whale are right up there along with Noah's ark and David and Goliath.

For those of us brought up in a Christian context, Jonah is part of our background biblical landscape. But then we grow up and wonder: who could survive being swallowed by a fish? And in enough health to then preach to a city? How could a whole nation repent? Would a plant grow up overnight? How can we believe that the story of Jonah is historical? Surely it is a parable or allegory – isn't it written in a story form?

For those of us who have come to faith later in life, perhaps there are similar questions. Every time we engage with the Bible, we can only gain by wrestling with difficult issues. I have no desire to be controversial; just honest.

For some of us, questions of historicity are not a problem, either because it is good enough for us that the book of Jonah seems to be presented as history in the Old Testament, or because we are more focused on what it may be teaching.

For those who are wondering, may I suggest a bit of 'digging' in a Bible commentary or two? A few pointers might be that there are no comparable allegorical writings in contemporary Jewish literature; there is no explanation if it is a parable; evidence exists that Nineveh experienced religious reform around 800BC; and Jesus talked about Jonah as history (Matthew 12:41). On the other hand, we have no other reliable confirmation that surviving a fish internment is possible.

Whatever we conclude, our priority is not to answer these questions definitively. It is to engage with the God with whom Jonah engaged. There are too many riches to discover to thrash about for long in the stormy waters of theological debate. If you have never read Jonah through, give yourself a few minutes to do that. It won't take long. Let's see where we land.

Disobeying

The word of the Lord came to Jonah son of Amittai: 'Go to the great city of Nineveh and preach against it, because its wickedness has come up before me.' But Jonah ran away from the Lord and headed for Tarshish. (NIV)

Some background to the story: Jonah was a prophet in the northern kingdom of Israel, living around 800 years before Jesus, and a contemporary of other prophets like Elisha, Amos and Hosea. He was clearly a notable figure, with the ear of the king. Jonah correctly prophesied that King Jeroboam would restore Israel's northern borders with Assyria, ending the conflict between the two nations (2 Kings 14:25). The newly established security enabled the northern kingdom to flourish. This turned out to be a bit of a mixed blessing, as the people began to take God for granted. Amos and Hosea proclaimed that Israel was under God's judgement for this complacency, and it would result in exile to the dreaded Assyria.

It was in the middle of this serious national situation that Jonah was suddenly commanded by God to go off into enemy territory, to Assyria's capital city no less, in order to declare judgement on the Assyrians as well and invite them to repent.

This was clearly not in the least what Jonah wanted to do. It was an ultimate 'Really, God?' moment. Jonah had a good prophetic track record in Israel, with his most famous prophecy being against mighty Assyria. No wonder he ran away from this commission. Never mind the risk to life and limb, Jonah absolutely did not want God to offer grace to Israel's enemies. Surely Israel was beloved of God, not Assyria. How dare God extend his love beyond Israel; how could he blur the boundaries in this way? Wasn't Israel 'in' with God, and Assyria 'out'? And worst of all – if the Assyrians repented, if God had mercy, if catastrophic judgement was averted after Jonah had prophesied its imminent arrival, then what would that do to Jonah's reputation as a prophet? It could ruin him. There was too much at stake for him, professionally and spiritually. Time to run.

Tarshish was about as far away from Nineveh as you could get in those days. Have you ever run away from God? What happened? Do you know why you did it? Is there any unfinished business you need to sort out?

DIANA ARCHER

Running

Then the Lord sent a great wind on the sea, and such a violent storm arose that the ship threatened to break up. All the sailors were afraid and each cried out to his own god. And they threw the cargo into the sea to lighten the ship. (NIV)

Jonah had barely collapsed on to his bunk bed, after all the rush to board at Joppa, before the ship he chose was flung into a nasty storm. He was oblivious – he was below deck in exhaustion. But there was great consternation above him. Sailors are not easily scared, but this storm was something else. A mixed bunch of nationalities and origins, these experienced sea-goers were turning to a variety of gods in desperate fear. But it was none of their objects of worship who were responsible for their dire straits. In trying to avoid bringing grace to his enemies, Jonah achieved more than he intended by putting the sailors in mortal danger. For it was God himself who sent the wind.

And so we too are thrown into complicated questions about God's sovereignty over nature, and his actions in response to one prophet's disobedience. If God sent the wind, then he must have cared enough for those Ninevites to chase Jonah down and demand his attention in a most extreme way. A whole ship's crew was endangered, along with their passenger. Jonah was not going to get away with desertion.

Does this mean that the storms of life come along because we are being disobedient? If things go wrong, is it because we are doing wrong? Do we effectively bring suffering upon ourselves?

I guess there may be times when, in fact, we do. We can't, for example, escape into addictive behaviours without bringing negative consequences upon ourselves. But are unhappy circumstances necessarily the response of God to us getting it all wrong? Many have created their own internal storms by blaming themselves for illness, disaster and challenges. How do we know if we are like Jonah, in need of redemption, or just normal people living in a pain-ridden world?

Read Romans 5:1–5.

DIANA ARCHER

Hiding

But Jonah had gone below deck, where he lay down and fell into a deep sleep. The captain went to him and said, 'How can you sleep? Get up and call on your god! Maybe he will take notice of us so that we will not perish.' (NIV)

There are various ways to deal with seemingly overwhelming challenges. One of them is simply to bury ourselves away from them and live in denial. While the sailors recognised the danger they were in and attempted to respond practically and spiritually, Jonah determinedly went to sleep.

Let's face it: Jonah had been asked to do a pretty difficult task. Offering grace and kindness to our enemies, especially to those who would not think twice about lopping off our heads, is no small thing.

Just pause and think about that for a moment. Whom would you regard as your enemy or enemies? Where is your Nineveh? Would you willingly go and tell your Ninevites about the good news of God's grace, embodied ultimately in Jesus? It's not an easy thought. Our Nineveh may be our workplace, the school gate, our families, our neighbours – probably not physically dangerous, but still seemingly hostile to talk of God. Our enemy may be that person who clearly dislikes, bullies, ignores or belittles you. Or perhaps for you, declaring yourself a Christian would be potentially life-threatening. Who is your enemy?

God understands all of that, just like he understood how Jonah felt. But his compassion for the city of Nineveh would not be thwarted. The Ninevites were reportedly a violent, cruel, unjust people, who indulged in prostitution, witchcraft and commercial exploitation (see Nahum 3). They did not deserve God's kindness. But that was not the point. God wanted to offer it. He would therefore not allow Jonah to escape on a boat, or into a self-imposed stupor. He sent the ship's captain to wake him up and ask him the awkward questions. God faced Jonah with the truth of his disobedience and its devastating effect both on a boatload of sailors and on one of the most influential cities of the day.

In what ways was God showing kindness to Jonah in pulling him out of denial?

DIANA ARCHER

Owning up

[Jonah] answered, 'I am a Hebrew and I worship the Lord, the God of heaven, who made the sea and the dry land… Pick me up and throw me into the sea,' he replied, 'and it will become calm. I know that it is my fault that this great storm has come upon you.' (NIV)

A moment of truth at last. Jonah could not deny his desertion any longer. The sailors did not question that he was responsible for the storm. They understood that the God who made land and sea was the greatest, far beyond the smaller gods attached to the nations.

So Jonah took the blame. Yet even now, he did not obey God. He could have said, 'Yes, this storm is my fault. I will repent, and go to Nineveh. Put me on the first boat back again once we land.' But he decided he would rather die than do that. Extraordinary.

Is he the only one? What lengths will we go to in order to avoid God's way of doing things? Why is it that we think we know best, even though rationally we know that God is God and we are not? Why is it so hard to give up cherished ways of thinking and open ourselves to God's truth? It matters not where we start – whether we challenge God in out-and-out rebellion like Jonah, or feel that we are unloved, undeserving and have the lowest self-esteem. Wherever we are, when our feelings and perceived evidence tell us one thing, it is so very difficult to hear another message. Is it because, at our deepest levels, we fear change – we fear what might happen? We fear it might be painful (it might). We fear we might be proved wrong (we might). We fear it will have scary implications (very likely). We fear we won't be okay (unlikely). We fear that God does not know best (he does!).

Yet Jesus said, 'If you hold to my teaching, you are really my disciples. Then you will know the truth, and the truth will set you free' (John 8:31–32). Who will you believe?

If Jonah had not owned up, what might have happened? Read 1 John 4:18.

DIANA ARCHER

Courage

Instead, the men did their best to row back to land. But they could not, for the sea grew even wilder than before… Then they took Jonah and threw him overboard, and the raging sea grew calm. At this the men greatly feared the Lord. (NIV)

Well now, what nice guys these sailors were. Unlike Jonah, who ran away from offering kindness to the Ninevites, the sailors tried their absolute best to save his life, despite the perilous situation. The contrast between their actions and Jonah's could not have been greater. While the esteemed prophet was sabotaging his CV, these pagan seafarers were proving themselves of better character.

Did Jonah notice how much nicer they were than him? Was this part of the lesson he was supposed to learn – that his standing with God was not as firm as he thought? Here were non-Hebrews outpacing him in kindness and sacrifice. He had not been prepared to put his life on the line for the Ninevites, but the sailors were prepared to endure extreme danger for him. Was Jonah aware that God was punching holes in his assumptions again? Perhaps the people of God did not have a monopoly on being and doing the right thing after all.

Jesus spent a lot of his time trying to say similar things in his day to those who assumed they were favoured by God. He offended many of the religious elite, especially scribes and Pharisees, by challenging their sense of being in the right, and their consequent oppression of other people who they thought in the wrong. Being a descendant of Abraham was not good enough for Jesus. Only believing in the one whom God had sent would do.

And us? How many times have we maligned others who think differently from us, whether within or outside of the Christian community? Belonging to Jesus does not automatically make us instantly kinder, nicer or more right. That's a journey we take with the Holy Spirit. In the meantime, it may well be that others are simply more Jesus-like than we are.

Read John 8:31–59.

DIANA ARCHER

Into the deep

Now the Lord provided a huge fish to swallow Jonah, and Jonah was in the belly of the fish three days and three nights. (NIV)

Now for the fish. Do you believe that God is sovereign over the elements? Do you think that he wound up the world and set it going, and left it to run on without his interference? Does he ever 'break' his own rules of gravity, atmospheric pressure and weather patterns? We know so much more than Jonah did about how beyond our imagination the cosmos is: how incredible the galaxies, how small our planet Earth, how beautiful the universe. Yet still we wonder – would God, could God, have kept a man inside a fish?

It's rather a key part to the story. Nothing really works without it. No storm-calming. No sailors having a revelation that Jonah's God was worth worshipping. No rescue of Jonah. No hope for the Ninevites. It's crazy enough to be true.

The resonances with the gospels are also vital. Jesus took Jonah seriously. In sparring with the Pharisees and teachers of the law, Jesus responded to frustrating challenges to his authority by saying that the 'sign of Jonah' would be the one they would get – comparing the ready repentance of the Ninevites with the reluctance of the religious elite to see the truth in him. He declared that something 'greater than Jonah' was there, and yet few could recognise it. He compared Jonah's three-day ordeal within the fish, and subsequent rescue, with the Son of Man's upcoming three days 'in the heart of the earth' after crucifixion (Matthew 12:38–41). Jonah returned. Would the Pharisees work out that Jesus would too?

The story of Jonah is against all expectations and odds. In order to bring the offer of repentance and redemption and experience of God's grace, so is the story of Jesus.

Father, help me to see you more as you really are. Help me to be open to the truth.

DIANA ARCHER

Fishy prayers

'In my distress I called to the Lord, and he answered me. From deep in the realm of the dead I called for help, and you listened to my cry… I said, "I have been banished from your sight; yet I will look again towards your holy temple."' (NIV)

Presumably Jonah had no expectation of anything but a miserable death as he flew through the air and into the raging waves. Even inside the fish, he did not know what would happen next. Was this a temporary reprieve? Would he end his days in stomach acid rather than salt water? Yet Jonah seemed aware that he was in the middle of a miraculous rescue. His previous rebellion had proved no match for his almighty God. He had been tracked down, challenged and found wanting. But, as he sank into the depths and finally turned to God for help, he was saved from a watery grave.

Jonah knew that he deserved punishment – to be 'banished' from God's sight (v. 4) for his disobedience. But he chose to turn back to God. His cry for mercy was answered by the redemptive grace of God. The grace he did not want to offer to others was given to him in full measure.

It doesn't matter how far we have gone from God; it doesn't matter what we have done or how badly we feel about ourselves. Thankfully there is, as Psalm 139:7–12 says, nowhere we can go that is too far for God to come and meet us with his limitless grace.

In his psalm-like prayer, Jonah made the choice to engage with God again, and his life was saved, albeit in an extremely unexpected way. This is the character of the God we worship – a God who declares himself as 'slow to anger, abounding in love and forgiving sin and rebellion' (Numbers 14:18). It may be that his rescue of us is not what we thought it would be. It may be uncomfortable, challenging and not what we wanted. But God always responds to us when we turn to him. Always.

God's grace reached out to Jonah to rescue him from himself. Has anyone ever done that for you? Have you ever thanked them?

DIANA ARCHER

Worshipping

'Those who cling to worthless idols turn away from God's love for them. But I, with shouts of grateful praise, will sacrifice to you. What I have vowed I will make good. I will say, "Salvation comes from the Lord."' (NIV)

It is wonderful that Jonah could make all these promises and declare God's goodness while he was still inside the fish. His complete redemption had not yet happened, but his change of heart and mind looked complete. He was back on God's agenda, full of praise for the Almighty and determined to fulfil his commission. His faith was on the rise again, and he was already thanking God for what he would do next.

But wait – that 'worthless idols' bit. Jonah himself had clung to his idolatrous rebellion instead of trusting God. Yet this sounds like he was talking about other people, not himself. Did he still have some lessons to learn? Had Jonah not made the connections between his own behaviour, the grace of God and the Ninevites that God wanted to rescue as well? While praising God for his own rescue, Jonah still poured contempt on those who refused God's love, rather than compassion.

It was easy for Jonah to see how nations other than Israel worshipped 'worthless idols', for they were artisan-made of wood and stone. They sat in temples, on shelves in the home or were carried on travels. They were offered sacrifices, which ranged from pieces of fruit to young children, and were generally to be feared and placated. They were one of the reasons that Israel was commanded not to make images of God.

It is harder for us to see idols that we or others might worship. We may not intend to turn away from God's love, but things do compete for it: things like success, independence, family, money, power, looks, fitness, having-it-all-together. All these can demand our loyalty over and above our relationship with God. And yes, we still make stuff from wood and stone – and metal and plastic and concrete – that eats up our time, money, attention and love.

Let's try not to make Jonah's mistake of criticising the foolishness of others while ignoring our own compromises. The words 'speck', 'eye' and 'plank' spring to mind.

DIANA ARCHER

The day of reckoning

Jonah obeyed the word of the Lord and went to Nineveh… Jonah began by going a day's journey into the city, proclaiming, 'Forty more days and Nineveh will be overthrown.' The Ninevites believed God. A fast was proclaimed, and all of them, from the greatest to the least, put on sackcloth. (NIV)

When my husband and I were missionaries in Japan, many moons ago, we lived in the large city of Kobe, in the mission headquarters. On the kitchen wall was a calendar, with a verse for each day. We will always remember the morning we looked at it to find, 'And God spake to the fish.' I have to confess we struggled to apply it to our day's challenges, but it did refresh our sense of humour.

But Jonah needed rescuing again. There he was, vomited on to dry land. Let's hope he had a wash and a change of clothes before he set off on his long journey to Nineveh. The following verse is easier to apply, for Jonah was recommissioned. God renewed his command to Jonah, and this time, Jonah obeyed. How brilliant is our God, that he does not write us off when we fall at the first hurdle – or the second, or the third! Generally speaking, the world wants us to get it right first time – indeed, *we* want to get it right first time. Neither the world nor we are patient with failure. But God is entirely different. He will restore us again, and again, and again. He will teach us, again and again. Never think that you are beyond the pale. He loves you.

Nineveh at last. Perhaps now Jonah would see why God was so keen to get him there. This enormous city, which took three days to walk through, was ripe for the picking. Jonah barely had to open his mouth, and the Ninevites repented in droves. Perhaps his reputation as a prophet was still intact after all. Perhaps God's Spirit had been working on hearts and minds so that they were ready. Perhaps God did know best all along.

If God can rescue Jonah from drowning, via a fish, he can rescue you when you need it. And we all do need it. Who knows who else will benefit from God's grace to you?

DIANA ARCHER

Even the king

'Let people and animals be covered with sackcloth. Let everyone call urgently on God. Let them give up their evil ways and their violence. Who knows? God may yet relent and with compassion turn from his fierce anger so that we will not perish.' (NIV)

The spiritual 'capture' of Nineveh was complete, once the king heard of Jonah and his message. The king of Assyria responded just like everyone else, and then turned this heart-response into a law: everyone was to repent. The Ninevites showed their intention to change their ways in symbolic forms that were recognisable to Jonah: they fasted from food and drink, they took off fancy clothes and wore basic sackcloth, and they prayed like mad. They even made their animals fast as well, perhaps as a sign of their commitment, for they would have been dependent on them for food, livelihood and travel. And while I can't imagine tying sackcloth to my dog, I get the point. The Ninevites were wholehearted in their repentance.

So, what if we have been behaving like those Ninevites? What if our hearts, minds and behaviour have been straying far from God, and we know it? Do we want to wait for a wakeup call, like a fish or a prophet? Or shall we take the initiative and face up to what we have been doing?

It might help to remember that God does understand why we run away or behave badly. He made us with needs that are to be met – it's the way we go about that which is so crucial. Another prophet expressed God's agony about the way we run after things that cannot satisfy, rather than turning to him (Jeremiah 2:13). God, our heavenly Father, is the only one who knows us, loves us completely and can genuinely meet our needs. He is the only one who is eternal, and he can be eternally trusted.

The story of salvation is essentially a love story between God and us, ultimately expressed through Jesus Christ. Don't believe that anything else can give you what he can.

The Ninevites wore sackcloth and sat in the dust. How would God know if you were changing your ways and calling to him for mercy?

DIANA ARCHER

Responding to grace

When God saw what they did and how they turned from their evil ways, he relented and did not bring on them the destruction he had threatened. (NIV)

This is probably the most dramatic turning point in this dramatic story. It's bigger than Jonah's extraordinary experience, bigger than the storm, the sailors and the fish. This was what God had been aiming at all along. While Jonah had been sent to declare judgement on the Ninevites, the reason for this was because God wanted to treat them with grace.

God's judgement is always about grace. The reason for declaring the sins of the nation of Assyria, typified in its capital city of Nineveh, was to give them the chance to turn away from them. It was not to condemn them, but rather to give the chance to repent. If they acknowledged their wrongdoing, their 'evil' and violent ways, God could forgive them. It was his heart of love reaching out to Nineveh that God wanted Jonah to convey. The Old Testament is stacked with similar messages, mostly to God's own people, the Israelites, but also to many of the surrounding nations. Listen to the truth, said the prophets. Listen, agree, repent. Change your ways, put God first. It matters! Grace is there for you if only you will bend the knee.

Do we need backing up against a wall before we will give in? Perhaps that depends on our personality. Some of us are more defensive than others. Some of us will fight on and on to prove ourselves right. But the point is that God is always right and in the right. And if we care about being right with him, his way is really the only way. We must get ourselves off the throne and let him be king. His word is eternally true; ours is flawed and patchy at best. Don the sackcloth and then enjoy your heavenly Father's extraordinary grace.

Father, I don't mean to fight you. Indeed, I can easily beat myself up without your help. But teach me, by your Spirit, as you have promised. Lead me into truth about myself and you.

DIANA ARCHER

Forgiveness?

But to Jonah this seemed very wrong, and he became angry. He prayed to the Lord, 'Isn't this what I said, Lord, when I was still at home? That is what I tried to forestall by fleeing to Tarshish.' (NIV)

You have got to love this guy. After all he had been through, you would think that he had learned enough about the character of God to be absolutely delighted that Nineveh was to be spared. But no, Jonah was just furious.

Perhaps it is understandable. He had put his life and his reputation on the line for this city. And now it was going to be let off. There is something rather familiar about his response: 'God, I knew this was going to happen. I knew you were going to be nice. I just knew that you weren't going to give them what they clearly deserved. How could you? Now do you see why Tarshish was a great idea. I am done here.'

Have you ever had to forgive someone who has hurt you deeply? It is often hard to forgive them for making you feel angry, let alone for the original hurt. You never wanted to feel all these horrid emotions; your heart and head (and often digestive system) are in a mess. You would rather go back to those 'Lord, smash their teeth in' psalms (e.g. Psalm 58) than consider forgiveness. I have been there. We all have. I imagine that Jonah felt something like that. He wanted the Ninevites to get their come-uppance. Basically, this just wasn't fair.

It is hard to forgive. It is hard to know that God has forgiven, when you are still struggling to. God could do it; Jonah couldn't. He could not get to the bigger picture – he could not see that God's justice includes mercy. He could not rejoice that a whole city had been saved from destruction; he was just too deeply lost in his own reactions. He actually wanted to die.

If you are wrestling with unforgiveness, just ask God to help you. He will show the way. If you need to ask for forgiveness, then don't put it off a moment longer.

DIANA ARCHER

The right to be angry?

Jonah had gone out and sat down at a place east of the city. There he made himself a shelter, sat in its shade and waited to see what would happen to the city. (NIV)

Wouldn't it have been great if Jonah had stayed in the city to lead the people in repentance, gratitude and joy that their destruction had been averted? He could have stayed there to teach them new ways, and told them more about the God to whom they were praying. But no, Jonah stomped off in disgust, because he already knew that God had relented. Jonah's anger had taken over.

So we find him sitting in the shade, hoping against hope that God might still destroy his enemies' city. He was consumed with anger, raging against God and his plans, and unable to relate to God's love and compassion for the Ninevites. It seems that God added fuel to the fire, by first causing a plant to protect Jonah from the extreme heat, and then taking it away again. That just made Jonah even more cross. And God asked him the same question a second time: 'Is it right for you to be angry?'

Now that is a question. Jonah thought that he had a perfect right to anger. How could God show grace to a people who had consistently opposed, fought with and endangered the nation of Israel? This was all topsy-turvy and inside-out. But anger has its own internal self-justification. When we are angry, we are usually absolutely sure that we have a right to it. It is near impossible to see another point of view. Like Jonah, we can be blindingly furious.

Or perhaps we come in from the other end. We have pushed anger so far out of our range that we don't even know when it is there, and would probably have thanked God for sending the plant-eating worm. That isn't any healthier. Anger at injustice of any sort may be extremely necessary and we may need its motivational energy.

Have you any right to be angry? What will you do?

DIANA ARCHER

Amazing grace

But the Lord said… 'Should I not have concern for the great city of Nineveh, in which there are more than a hundred and twenty thousand people who cannot tell their right hand from their left – and also many animals?' (NIV)

So now we come full circle. This is where the story of Jonah began – with God's heart of compassion and love for Nineveh – and this is where it ends. We don't know what happened next to Jonah. Perhaps a few days in the heat melted his anger, and he went back to Israel with a wider understanding of God's love. Perhaps he didn't. We are left with the question that God asked him.

Should God not be concerned about our enemies? Should he favour those of us who know we belong to him? Whose side is he actually on?

I find the way that the Ninevites are described quite moving – God talks about them as people who do not know their right hand from their left. God had compassion because these people did not know any better. They did not know how to live. No one had told them. When they heard the message of coming judgement, they were appalled – they had not realised what they were doing.

It often seems as if those who commit obviously evil acts are 'evil' through and through. Certainly that is how they are described in the media. But perhaps some have never known how not to be like this. Perhaps, like the Ninevites, no one ever told them. Their bad choices have led from one awful consequence to another, and it's never-ending. Rather than condemn them out of hand, one of the messages from the story of Jonah is the invitation to see the world as God does: with compassion. God sees us all. He sees our hearts – he sees what is behind and beneath our actions. He has extended his grace to us, and he sends us, like Jonah, to extend it to others.

'When [Jesus] saw the crowds, he had compassion on them, because they were harassed and helpless, like sheep without a shepherd' (Matthew 9:36).
DIANA ARCHER

Joy spilling out: Philippians

Christine Platt writes:

Philippians is a happy letter. The writer, Paul, is in prison, but not having a pity party. Instead, he is joyous and buoyant. He urges the Philippians – and, by extension, us – to find joy and to express joy in all our circumstances. The best evidence indicates that Paul was in Rome under house arrest (Acts 28:30–31), so he faced the curtailment of his freedom yet was able to share Jesus with all who came to see him.

His pastoral heart urged him to visit the Philippian church and all the other churches in the region to encourage and instruct them in God's ways, but that was no longer possible. He didn't angrily protest the injustice of his imprisonment, but came to a place of calm confidence and delight in his relationship with God and his plans for his life. If God thought it was best for him to be in Rome and unable to visit his flock, then Paul rested in that reality. How often I fret and get into a tizz when things don't work out. Rather than calm confidence and delight, I flap around like a demented hen!

Several years ago, due to a visa misunderstanding, I was locked up in a dirty mosquito-infested room by immigration officials in Nigeria prior to being deported back to the UK. I confess I was hopping mad rather than peaceful and confident in God's perfect plan. However, over the following few weeks, I began to see God use that situation significantly to develop the ministry I was involved with in Nigeria. So, he did know best!

Paul's joy spilling out under such testing would have been a huge encouragement to his readers who were also undergoing trying situations. And so we too can understand that it is possible to be serene and joyous even when all is seemingly going wrong. Paul is following the example of the master, Jesus. On Palm Sunday, Jesus was praised as a noble teacher who came in the name of the Lord. By the following Friday, he was hanging on a cross. He faced all that with quiet assurance in the Father's will and purpose: 'for the joy set before him he endured the cross' (Hebrews 12:2, NIV).

Let us learn to live each day with such confident joy-filled faith.

Praying with joy

In all my prayers for all of you, I always pray with joy... he who began a good work in you will carry it on to completion until the day of Christ Jesus. (NIV)

Is praying for others a joy for you or sometimes more of a chore? Every time Paul thought about the Philippians, he gave thanks to God and prayed with joy. The church in Philippi would have been full of fallible human beings, so I'm sure not everything was sweetness and light! Despite inevitable disappointments, Paul chose to focus on what God was doing, not the shortcomings of the people. God had initiated his work in their lives and he always finishes what he starts.

Could it be that in our prayers we focus on problems and what is going wrong, rather than what is going well or what God has promised for our family, friends and neighbours? Our gracious God is always actively at work in his world. He will always strive to bring about good in people's lives until their last breath. It may not always be obvious, but God says he will 'carry it on to completion' so we can be sure he will. All those for whom we pray have the same access to God if they choose to position themselves to receive it. So we can pray with joy and thanks because of who God is and what he promises. He points out: 'I am the Lord, the God of all [humankind]. Is anything too hard for me?' (Jeremiah 32:27). No heart is too stony or mind so closed that God cannot get through and turn people around.

I confess I get exasperated at people's stubbornness, stumbling along in life pursuing empty dreams, and I am tempted to give up on them. But God never gives up and neither did Paul. I want to learn to lift my mind above the everyday difficulties and pray more God-shaped prayers which will surely generate more joy.

Mighty Lord Jesus – I thank you for my friends, family and neighbours and I look forward to seeing you working in their lives so they will please you and be a light for you in this world.

CHRISTINE PLATT

Gain through loss

My imprisonment here has had the opposite of its intended effect. Instead of being squelched, the Message has actually prospered. All the soldiers here… found out that I'm in jail because of this Messiah. That piqued their curiosity, and now they've learned all about him. (MSG)

Romans 8:28 states, 'We can be so sure that every detail in our lives of love for God is worked into something good.' This verse can be hard to accept, especially if it's shared with us in times of deep pain. We need to be certain of the Holy Spirit's prompting before we bring this verse to others in crisis. Timing is crucial. However, this situation with Paul is a beautiful example of the truth of it. God can and does bring good out of everything that happens to us. It may take time, but it will come.

Paul had limitations forced upon him. He couldn't travel to do his pastoral and evangelistic work – how frustrating! But God gave him a different captive audience: the soldiers. Many of us have limitations thrust upon us through illness, family responsibilities and financial constraints. This reading is particularly pertinent for me. Right now, I'm struggling to adjust to the limitations that age is forcing on me. I have less energy and strength, so am grieving the loss of capacity to get through my to-do list! And I know it's only going to get worse as I get older. I need to deal with this now, otherwise I'll face years of sadness, frustration and disappointment.

From a narrowing of life's opportunities, Paul was able to see God giving him different ways to serve. Without his times in prison, Paul would probably never have written his letters; so much of the New Testament would be missing – wow! Paul wouldn't have known the ongoing significance of his letters, but I bet now, from the perspective of heaven, he's very glad he wrote them – and so am I!

Write out Romans 8:28 and put it where you will see it often. Ask God to help you see life from this perspective whenever things don't go as you'd hoped.

CHRISTINE PLATT

What's on your bucket list?

I trust that my life will bring honor to Christ, whether I live or die. For to me, living means living for Christ, and dying is even better. But if I live, I can do more fruitful work for Christ. (NLT)

Have you ever had a near-death experience? I once was in danger of drowning, but was fortunately rescued. On the beach, as I tried to recover my breath, I realised that at that moment I could have been in heaven – which was very appealing. However, it reinforced to me that God had a reason for giving me more time. Many people find those experiences put life in perspective. Facing the imminent prospect of dying, yet escaping death's clutches and being granted more time, gives people a new outlook, a new appreciation and a new impetus to make every moment count. In the film *The Bucket List* (2007), Jack Nicholson and Morgan Freeman play two characters with terminal cancer. They decide to escape the hospital, indulge in wild adventures and fulfil long-held dreams. What would you do?

Paul faced life-and-death issues every day. His captors could have chopped off his head at any moment. He had no guarantee of a long life – and neither do we. Newspaper headlines report tragedy after tragedy, lives ending very abruptly with no warning. Those people don't get the opportunity to fulfil their bucket lists or to assess their life goals.

We would be wise to live according to Paul's motto: 'For to me living means living for Christ, and dying is even better. But if I live, I can do more fruitful work for Christ.' A short life lived for Christ is not a tragedy, whereas a long life lived without Jesus is a waste.

Paul's bucket list was to honour Christ and to do fruitful work for him, and we can all do that every day. We would then come to the end of our lives with no regrets, only the exhilarating prospect of being with Jesus forever.

In what ways can you honour Christ today and do fruitful work for him? This could be in your prayer life, family life, work life or in your community. Make the most of the moment.

CHRISTINE PLATT

It's a privilege!

For you have been given not only the privilege of trusting in Christ but also the privilege of suffering for him. We are in this struggle together. (NLT)

Try to imagine what it must feel like to dread a knock on the door, a visit from the secret police, to be hauled off to prison and threatened with torture and death until you renounced your faith in Jesus. I hope I would be brave. Millions of believers live in countries hostile to belief in Jesus. They are suffering just as Paul and the Philippians did. How privileged are those of us who can meet freely for worship and speak openly about our experience with God! It is easy to take that for granted, but we should thank God daily for our freedom and also pray for our persecuted brothers and sisters.

Many of us will probably never experience imprisonment or torture for our beliefs. For us, the opposition may be subtler. Paul tells us that suffering for Christ is a gift to be received, not to resent or to shy away from. One day at work, some of my colleagues ridiculed another's faith in God. I was quite shocked and couldn't think of anything to say. The moment passed, and I knew I had missed an opportunity. I fear I was more concerned about what they would think of me, than I was about taking the plunge to speak boldly for Christ and nail my colours to the mast. I want to make sure I step up next time.

In increasingly secularised societies, God is getting relegated to the sidelines. We need to bring him back into the mainstream. Let's embrace the privilege of suffering for him even if it means being misunderstood, teased or ostracised. Suffering is part of the package. We are Jesus people – we trust and we suffer.

Mighty Jesus, I pray for the persecuted church. Give them boldness and wisdom. Help me also to be courageous. Give me words to say to my family, my neighbours and colleagues that would stimulate interest in you.

CHRISTINE PLATT

It all comes from Jesus

If you've gotten anything at all out of following Christ, if his love has made any difference in your life, if being in a community of the Spirit means anything to you… love each other… Forget yourselves long enough to lend a helping hand. (MSG)

What have you gained from following Christ? Has his love made any difference in your life? Do Christian friends enrich your daily experience? These are insightful questions to ask, especially when we struggle to love and serve others in the way God asks us to.

Anything we can offer to anyone else – love, care, service, encouragement – all have their roots in him, not in our own reservoirs of goodness. If you are anything like me, your own capacity to love and care for others needs constant topping up with resources from Jesus.

Corrie ten Boom illustrates this beautifully. She and her family suffered grievously at the hands of the Nazis in World War II. After the war, one of the most vicious concentration camp guards approached her and asked for forgiveness. In that moment, Corrie knew she could not do it alone. She breathed a silent prayer for help. Love for this man flooded her whole being. She was able to warmly shake his hand and assure him of full and complete forgiveness. That takes my breath away.

This reading has brought to mind a few people who have made life more difficult for me in recent days. I'm tempted to nurse my resentment and sense of injustice. Only when the love of Jesus flows through my veins am I able to forgive and let it go. The wonderful thing about Jesus' love is that it is unending, and his reservoirs never run dry. 'God's loyal love couldn't have run out, his merciful love couldn't have dried up. They're created new every morning. How great your faithfulness! I'm sticking with God… He's all I've got left' (Lamentations 3:22–23).

Dip deep today into Jesus' loyal and merciful love. Experience it for yourself so that you can show mercy and love to all whom you meet, especially the more difficult people.

CHRISTINE PLATT

From humiliation to highest honour

Though he was God… he gave up his divine privileges; he took the humble position of a slave and was born as a human being… God elevated him to the place of highest honor… that at the name of Jesus every knee should bow. (NLT)

We know that Jesus experienced the utmost humiliation at the cross – his arrest, the soldiers' mockery, the false accusations, hanging virtually naked in front of a jeering crowd. But his whole life was evidence of chosen humility. Born under a moral cloud to a poor family, he lived the hard life of a manual worker for 30 years until the time came for him to reveal his true identity. As we know, that certainly didn't go smoothly. But now he is in the place of highest honour and one day, maybe very soon, he will receive praise and adoration from all humanity. All will bow the knee, whether willingly or not.

In lesser ways, human experience reflects his suffering; life's journey is often tainted with pain and grief and humiliation. But we weren't meant to live in a pain-filled world. God created a stunningly beautiful world – no plastic in his ocean, abundant resources for everyone, no hungry children, no poverty – just a rich life of loving God and each other. My heart yearns for that.

It all went horribly wrong and, try as we may, we can't make it all right. When one area of the world is brought out of war or famine, we breathe a sigh of relief. But before we've had a chance to relax, another crisis erupts elsewhere. These verses reassure us that one day it's all going to be okay – in fact, a lot more than okay! Jesus will come and make everything right. But how should we live in the interim?

Julian of Norwich (14th century) wrote: 'All shall be well, and all shall be well, and all manner of things shall be well.' She lived in a time of social upheaval in Britain as well as three outbreaks of the plague, so her life was not serene. But she was.

Do you sometimes feel overwhelmed by pain? Continue to make your contribution to alleviate suffering and be at peace. Remember that 'all shall be well'. Jesus will return and make everything right.

CHRISTINE PLATT

Candle power

Go out into the world uncorrupted, a breath of fresh air in this squalid and polluted society. Provide people with a glimpse of good living and of the living God. Carry the light-giving Message into the night. (MSG)

We're into winter and it's candle time again! I love the warm glow that candles give. Have you noticed during power cuts how much light comes from one small flame and how comforting that is when all around us is thick blackness? Even a tiny light helps us feel secure and find our way. When the darkness is deep and scary, the smallest pinprick of light is very welcome.

'It is better to light a single candle than to curse the darkness.' This quote has been attributed to several famous people, including Eleanor Roosevelt and Confucius, but it can also be inferred from Paul's teaching here.

We do live in a squalid and polluted society, but rather than shunning it and isolating ourselves safely behind our nice Christian fences, we are to take the light out there to provide people with a glimpse of good living and of the living God. If our light doesn't shine out, the world will only become darker still.

For some years, I regularly visited a prison in West Africa. It was exceedingly bleak – overcrowded, dark and smelly. As I sat with groups of inmates, we read the Bible, prayed and sang to God most high. I saw the darkness recede and the light of Jesus come in with rekindled hope in the prisoners' eyes and, for me, a fresh glimpse of God's compassion and power.

Listening to the news can be a depressing experience, but rather than 'cursing the darkness' – i.e. complaining about the government or society at large or the latest misdemeanours of wealthy corporate executives – we could pray and seek to bring God's light and power into the situation.

In what ways can you 'light a candle in the darkness' of your community, family or workplace? Ask God for ways to carry the light-giving Message into the night.

CHRISTINE PLATT

Sisters, workers, warriors

I thought I should send Epaphroditus back to you. He is a true brother, co-worker, and fellow soldier… He risked his life for the work of Christ. (NLT)

Epaphroditus is one of the lesser-known Bible characters, yet he was clearly a person of godly character who contributed significantly to the church and to Paul. There have been myriads of such people throughout history. They are not famous, have not had statues made in honour of them, have not written books or made memorable speeches. But his life is one to aspire to. He served energetically, even risked his life to assist Paul. After nearly dying, he got up from his sick bed and carried on serving.

I so appreciate the combination of Paul's commendation – brother, worker and soldier. There was a warm relationship as they served Jesus together. As a worker, he could be relied upon to do well whatever task was assigned, and he also showed the courage, discipline and endurance of a soldier.

Probably most of us will not find our names in the New Year's Honours List or have several million followers on Twitter. God's opinion is really all that matters. His glorious affirmation – 'Well done, my good and faithful servant' (Matthew 25:21) – is worth infinitely more than any human recognition.

Our world and the church today need many such good and faithful servants who quietly get on with what needs doing, who promote friendly relationships, who endure patiently under duress, who truly display the characteristics of sisters, brothers, workers and warriors, sometimes unnoticed except by God.

Paul urges the Philippians to receive Epaphroditus and 'welcome him in the Lord's love and with great joy, and give him the honor that people like him deserve' (v. 29). I hope they did. But if not, I'm sure Jesus welcomed him into heaven with delight when Epaphroditus finished his earthly race.

Take Jesus' words, 'Well done, my good and faithful servant', into your heart today and rest in his affirmation. Your contribution may seem small to you, but Jesus sees what it costs you and he is very pleased.

CHRISTINE PLATT

Grace under attack

Watch out for those… mutilators who say you must be circumcised to be saved. For we who worship by the Spirit of God are the ones who are truly circumcised. We rely on what Christ Jesus has done for us. We put no confidence in human effort. (NLT)

I meet many people these days who've had some Christian influence in their youth and even 'made a decision' to follow Christ. In adulthood, it has faded away. They've opted for a far less costly, and less meaningful, philosophy of life. 'I still believe in God and I'll live a good moral life – be kind to my neighbours etc., but I'll keep God in the background and I don't see the need to belong to a church. I'm sure God will be okay with that.'

In contrast, Paul's contemporaries were claiming that rigid obedience to the law was all that was required. 'Get circumcised, obey the law and God will be happy.' Paul knew all about the law and had been rigorous in obeying it. But when he encountered Jesus, the scales literally fell from his eyes and he understood that human effort was worthless: 'God saved you by his grace when you believed. And you can't take credit for this; it is a gift from God. Salvation is not a reward for the good things we have done, so none of us can boast about it' (Ephesians 2:8–9).

Working hard at Christian activities to clock up brownie points, or being a nice upstanding citizen – it's all outward show, not inner transformation. God looks at the heart and he looks for faith. We can't earn his love. He offers it freely. How arrogant humanity is to say, 'No thanks, I'll do it my way.' Because of our tendency to pride and self-will, it is hard to accept that without Jesus we are nothing and can do nothing to save ourselves. Let's do as Paul recommends and 'put no confidence in human effort' (v. 3).

The hymn 'Rock of ages' (Augustus M. Toplady) contains these memorable lines: 'Nothing in my hand I bring, simply to thy cross I cling.' Look up this hymn and allow these truths to liberate you from human effort for salvation.

CHRISTINE PLATT

Right to the end

I gave up all that inferior stuff so I could know Christ personally, experience his resurrection power, be a partner in his suffering, and go all the way with him to death itself. (MSG)

'O God, help me finish my earthly life well.' This prayer has been echoed by many through the centuries. As age and its limitations start to impinge on our physical abilities, there is a tendency for this to affect our spiritual enthusiasm. Paul is an older man now and knows his physical death, whether by execution or natural causes, draws closer.

He has no intention of plateauing. His ardent desire is to know Christ personally, experience his resurrection power, be a partner in his suffering, go all the way with him to death itself and enjoy the resurrection. I'm keen on all those – except being a partner in his suffering. That's not so appealing, especially when we consider the intense hardships and persecution that Paul experienced. Yet suffering seems to be part of the package. We serve a Saviour who suffered intensely. We can't expect to go through our lives with Christ without having experienced that hurt.

How did Paul cope with this on a daily basis? It seems one of his main motivations was to be raised with Christ after his physical death. 'If there was any way to get in on the resurrection from the dead, I wanted to do it' (v. 11).

All the deprivations and sorrow we encounter on earth will be more than compensated for when we meet Jesus in heaven. Our finite earthly lives are like the blink of an eye compared with eternity in a Christ-filled expanse. 'Death is gone for good – tears gone, crying gone, pain gone' (Revelation 21:4).

Let's not have any regrets about wasted years, gifts or opportunities. Let's make the most of all God has given, and face the fact that suffering will be part of that.

Lord, thank you for the priceless gift of eternity in heaven with you. Please remind me of this when I'm tempted to draw back from wholehearted obedience to you because of fear of suffering.

CHRISTINE PLATT

Don't dig up the past

I focus on this one thing: Forgetting the past and looking forward to what lies ahead, I press on to reach the end of the race and receive the heavenly prize for which God, through Christ Jesus, is calling us. (NLT)

I belong to a writers' group. When we critique each other's work, we have a rule to say two positive things and make one suggestion for improvement. Needless to say, most of us pay more attention to the suggestion for improvement rather than the praise. In life, many of us tend to focus on one negative comment and ignore lots of positive affirmation. We think about what's not so good rather than what's going great. That usually makes us feel fed up and discontented with ourselves.

If Paul had done that, he would never have lifted his chin from the mud. In contrast, he vowed to forget his past mistakes and look forward to the future. It can't have been easy. He had a lot to forget: he assented to Stephen being stoned and persecuted Christians mercilessly (Acts 8:1–3).

I'm certain Satan took every opportunity to remind Paul of his past in an attempt to discourage him. He does the same with us. Memories come back of our sins and blunders. Our accuser wants us to think about all the times we've failed, rather than be thankful for the many times we succeed.

God's desire is for us to place our mistakes and failures at the cross of Christ, claim his forgiveness and look forward, focusing on our strengths, victories and joys, not our weaknesses, losses and problems. Paul reminds us that 'we are citizens of heaven, where the Lord Jesus Christ lives. And we are eagerly waiting for him to return as our Saviour. He will take our weak mortal bodies and change them into glorious bodies like his own' (v. 20–21). What a marvellous prospect!

Merciful God, thank you that my sins and failures are buried in the sea of your forgiveness and there is a 'no fishing' sign. Help me live in that reality and resist the devil's attacks (see Ephesians 6:10–12).

CHRISTINE PLATT

Make your mind your friend

One final thing. Fix your thoughts on what is true, and honorable, and right, and pure, and lovely, and admirable. Think about things that are excellent and worthy of praise. (NLT)

At the end of most days, I have a short mental rerun of the day, thinking about who I've met and what I've done. I sometimes wonder what it would be like if I could remember each thought I'd had. How many would fit under Paul's headings – true, honourable, right, pure, lovely, admirable, excellent and worthy of praise?

One area that springs to mind is that, when listening to the national and world news, I get really irritated with some politicians and people of influence. I can waste a lot of precious mental energy berating them, and it doesn't help at all. Other times I get angry, sad and despondent when images of emaciated children or terrified refugees flit across the TV screen. How much healthier it would be if I prayed whenever I sense that irritation or sadness rising. After all, God is the only one who can really change things. That would be a more positive use of my brain cells rather than adrenalin shooting up my blood pressure about situations over which, humanly speaking, I have no control.

God has given us an amazingly capable and adaptable brain. This vast power house weighs about 1.3 kg (3 lbs), and yet it controls so much. As with any part of our body, we need to use it well and keep it as healthy as possible. Anger and bitterness poison the mind and will have detrimental physical effects on our bodies. Psychologists talk about making your mind your friend. Paul seems to be saying the same thing. It follows on from yesterday's reading about not dwelling on the negative but focusing on the positive. This is essential teaching for our world today.

Memorise this verse (Philippians 4:8) and ask for God's help to put it into practice. Thank God for the intricate and exceptional brain he has given you. Learn to take good care of it.

CHRISTINE PLATT

Recipe for contentment

I've found the recipe for being happy whether full or hungry, hands full or hands empty. Whatever I have, wherever I am, I can make it through anything in the One who makes me who I am. (MSG)

A wise person, sadly unknown, wrote: 'Discontentment makes rich people poor, while contentment makes poor people rich.'

You'd think that a person with a roof over their head and enough to eat would be content. But this is not the case. Human nature seems to yearn for a nicer roof and a tastier variety of food. The advertising industry feeds those desires.

Interestingly, I've observed that people in the developing world who live with the minimum of stuff sometimes express a greater level of contentment. I wonder if part of the reason is that they are not surrounded by shops full of delightful things or bombarded by ads for the latest 'essential' item. Maybe those of us in the developed world need to exercise more discipline, not get sucked into the whirlpool of materialism and resist the message of 'more, more, more'.

We can see that contentment doesn't come from outward resources but from an inner belief. Paul's recipe for being content whether in prison or free, with lots of food and comfort or none, was: 'Whatever I have, wherever I am, I can make it through anything in the One who makes me who I am.' He rested in God's provision for him.

Paul is not saying we should all take vows of poverty, although God may ask some to do that. Paul was also happy when he was well fed and adequately provided for. Whatever God gave, he accepted and was content.

Living this way could prove to be a radical lifestyle, which would demonstrate to a watching world that believers in Christ have discovered an important secret recipe. It could also free up more funds for those who are truly in need.

Are you ready for the challenge of displaying contentment with what God has provided for you? Take some time to think and pray over how this applies to you in your present circumstances.

CHRISTINE PLATT

Giving and receiving

Even when I was in Thessalonica you sent help more than once. I don't say this because I want a gift from you. Rather, I want you to receive a reward for your kindness. (NLT)

For about 20 years, I was in a similar situation to Paul in that I was dependent upon people giving me money so I could teach the Bible and point people to Christ, both in the UK and Africa. It's humbling to receive gifts and know that others have sacrificed some of their own resources so that I could do the job God had called me to. I love Paul's emphasis here. He is convinced that his financial supporters will receive a reward for their kindness, maybe in this life, but certainly in eternity.

This reminds me of a song by Ray Boltz called 'Thank you for giving to the Lord'. It tells the story of a new arrival in heaven being met by myriads of people thanking him/her for their gifts to missionaries and Christian workers, which made it possible for them to hear the good news and respond to the gospel. This is the magnificent reward.

The Philippian church would never have dreamt that their gifts to Paul would still be accruing them a reward two thousand years later, as people read Paul's letters and are encouraged in their faith. We too have no idea of the ripples of power and grace that flow out from our gifts to our needy world, but we can be sure that God takes note of them. Boltz's song goes on to say that many small and large sacrifices made are unnoticed on earth, but celebrated in heaven. Giving to build God's kingdom on earth is truly a stupendous investment, reaping unheard-of dividends. One day, we will stand in heaven flabbergasted at how God has multiplied our offering, and maybe we'll wish we'd given more.

Almighty God, my provider, thank you for the privilege of giving from what you have given me. Help me to be generous and wise in resourcing the growth of your kingdom on earth.

CHRISTINE PLATT

Water!

Lyndall Bywater writes:

When you think of the Middle East, there's a good chance you think of oil. After all, it's one of the main reasons for much of the unrest we've seen in the region over the past half-century. Yet there's a commodity that is far more precious and fought-over than oil, and that's water. Water is in desperately short supply in the Middle East and North Africa region. Seventeen countries fall below what's known as the 'Water poverty line', with 13 falling into the UN's 'Absolute water scarcity' category, meaning they don't have enough water for even the basic needs of their inhabitants. Some of this crisis is political – countries that do have enough water are unwilling to grant access to countries that don't – but much of it is geographical. The region contains just one per cent of the earth's water.

And it's in this region, made up of so much desert land, where the writers of the Bible lived. Perhaps it's no surprise, then, that they have a lot to say about water. After all, when something is precious and scarce, we think about it a lot. To most of us, water is just one of those things we take for granted, but in the Bible, water takes on a leading role. It floods and it blocks; it soothes and it heals; it revives and it transforms. It's never just one of those things – it's always a game changer.

The writers of the scriptures frequently use water as a symbol of God's presence. Of course, they talk about it as something that cleanses our bodies and slakes our thirst, but it is much more than that. Wherever water appears, the situation changes completely. Jesus did some interesting things with it too: everything from walking on it to turning it into wine. The message is clear: when you have water, things aren't the same anymore.

Geographically speaking, I may live in a land where water is plentiful – sometimes too plentiful – but spiritually I often feel as though I live in a desert. The people I meet in my local community are dry, surviving on just a trickle of peace and hope. Even those who follow Jesus are often getting by on the bare minimum. We may not need another rain shower any time soon, but we certainly do need to taste more of God's life-giving presence.

The sign of water

For as the waters fill the sea, the earth will be filled with an awareness of the glory of the Lord. (NLT)

Don't you just love the tipping point – that moment when a meeting becomes an encounter with God? It might happen during a prayer time or a worship song, but for me, it's usually when someone is telling their story. One minute I'm listening to someone recounting a series of events, then suddenly the atmosphere turns electric as their story brings to life something of the love and power of God. Of course, he's been there all along, but it's as though his presence suddenly becomes 'tangible'.

Habakkuk's words are thousands of years old, yet they seem timeless, don't they? Our world is still all too often an unjust place. It still feels as if we're waiting for God to make things right. So verse 14 comes as something of an encouragement. One day, the whole earth will be full of the knowledge, or the 'awareness', of God's glory. 'Glory' is a tricky word to grasp, but it might help to think of it as that 'tangible presence' that invades the room when you experience that tipping point I was describing earlier. True, the earth is already full of God – his loving presence filling every crevice of this world – but one day it'll actually feel like it.

If water is a picture of God's presence, then you might liken it to the water table – the store of water that is always there beneath our feet, real and sustaining but so often out of sight. One day, God's glorious presence will be as unmissable as a mighty ocean. You may cherish those encounters with God because they are relatively rare, but God's plan is that you should grow in your awareness of him until your life is awash with his glorious presence.

Water is the most ordinary thing, and it's all around us, which makes it a great reminder. Each time you see water today, stop to thank God that one day his presence will flood our world, making all things new.

LYNDALL BYWATER

Water in the desert

Water will gush forth in the wilderness and streams in the desert. The burning sand will become a pool, the thirsty ground bubbling springs. In the haunts where jackals once lay, grass and reeds and papyrus will grow. (NIV)

On my shelf I have a Selaginella Lepidophylla, otherwise known as a 'resurrection plant'. Most of the time it looks like a dried-up clump of grass, but if you give it a bit of water and then wait a few hours, it transforms. Its leaves unfurl, and it turns a healthy shade of green. The remarkable thing is that you can leave it without water for months – even years – and it will still come to life the next time it gets a drink.

If you were to read the book of Isaiah from start to finish, you could be forgiven for feeling rather depressed by the time you reached chapter 35. The prophecies in the first part of the book are warnings about what it's like when people and nations try to do life without God. There are accounts of evil rulers, terrifying monsters and ravaged landscapes.

And then there's chapter 35… and God's glory arrives. The prophecies of Habakkuk and Isaiah were given at similar times, and Isaiah uses that same image of water to depict what happens when God's presence becomes visible and tangible in a place – except in this prophecy it doesn't just fill the earth, but it changes the whole landscape. Water flows and life bursts forth. God's glory arrives, and everything changes.

Deserts are beautiful, complex ecosystems, and our earth needs them, but even the hardiest desert needs water from time to time. The desert seasons in our lives are important – we learn things there that we can't learn when everything's comfortable and easy – but we were not made to dwell there forever. We all need to know that no desert is too dry or too dead. With a few drops of God's glorious presence, life can spring up in our parched places.

Are you in a desert? Carry a bottle of water with you today. Whenever you feel discouraged or weary, pour some on to your hand. Feel its freshness and remember that God will one day bring your desert to life.

LYNDALL BYWATER

Water brings life

'This river flows east through the desert into the valley of the Dead Sea. The waters of this stream will make the salty waters of the Dead Sea fresh and pure. There will be swarms of living things wherever the water of this river flows.' (NLT)

The floor in our church once split open in the middle of a prayer meeting. It was very dramatic! There was a loud crack, and a whole line of tiles burst upwards. The explanation was depressingly mundane – something to do with the flooring having shifted since we removed the pews – but for us in that moment of welcoming God's presence, it was a powerful sign. It was as though he was telling us that he longed to break out of our tidy routines and our stifling structures.

There are many fascinating things to note from this story in Ezekiel, but the one I want to draw your attention to is the way that river keeps getting deeper the further it goes from the temple. I wonder if Ezekiel thought that strange. He would have known that water symbolised God's presence and glory, and he might logically have assumed that it would be at its deepest and fullest right there under the altar in the holiest place on earth. Surely it would get shallower and less powerful the further it went from the temple. But what he saw was a river that got deeper and deeper the further it went into the world, a river that transformed the whole landscape and brought vibrant life wherever it went. Are you starting to spot a theme?

We fall easily into the trap of thinking that God's presence will be most tangible and most powerful in church. After all, that's where God's people are. Yet God has never asked humanity to build him a building for his glory to hide out in. He never really wanted a temple in the first place. His Spirit is always longing to break out of our buildings and our meetings, to flow to the places that need life.

Stand a toilet roll tube in a bowl and hold it still as you pour water down into the tube. As you watch what happens, pray that God's presence will break out from your church and flow into the community.

LYNDALL BYWATER

Fresh water for a new day

'My people have committed two sins: They have forsaken me, the spring of living water, and have dug their own cisterns, broken cisterns that cannot hold water.' (NIV)

I've never journalled much, but I did have sporadic moments of diary-keeping when I was a teenager. I was reading a few of the entries recently and found myself simultaneously inspired and appalled: inspired because teenaged me had a vibrant faith that shaped my attitudes and choices, even at that young age; appalled because some of the things I believed about God and his character were so wrong.

God promised his people that they would be in relationship with him. Other nations worshipped gods who demanded to be feared. The Israelites worshipped a God who wanted to be known. He never intended them to 'learn' him like a subject in school. He meant them to drink from him like a fountain. Yet so often they didn't. They lived from leaky tanks of human understanding. They stored up their own good ideas instead of drinking fresh wisdom and strength from him.

I'm glad I'm not still living on that basic understanding I had of God in my teenage years. That water was fresh and life-giving at the time, but it would be stagnant now, and some of it might even be dangerous, since it was shot through with my adolescent belief that God couldn't love me if I didn't get things right. I'm glad I was taught to keep drinking from that fountain, because it meant I got to know more of who God is.

Are you living on old, stagnant revelation of God? Perhaps it seems a long time since you learnt anything new about him. Or perhaps, like me, you picked up some wrong views of God when you were young, and you know they still flavour your relationship with him. He longs to swap your stagnant water for fresh.

As you pray today, bring a glass of water and leave it out all day. When you come to pray tomorrow, empty the water and refill the glass as a reminder that God has fresh revelation for you to drink.

LYNDALL BYWATER

Drawing at the wells

With joy you will draw water from the wells of salvation. (NIV)

A friend of mine recently got a new puppy. At the end of a particularly fraught day, she sent me a desperate missive telling me how badly everything was going, and I replied with a few words of wisdom gleaned from over 25 years of dog ownership. The next time we met, she greeted me exuberantly and proclaimed: 'That text you sent me saved my life!'

Of course, I didn't literally save her life, but perhaps I was able to draw some help and hope from the wells of salvation for her.

In Bible times, drawing water from the well was often women's work. That's why Abraham's servant found Isaac's future wife Rebekah there (Genesis 24:10–15), and that's why, centuries later, Jesus found the Samaritan woman there (John 4:5–7). So the reference in today's reading to 'drawing water from the wells of salvation' would have had particular resonance for women. In fact, it might even have seemed strange that something as precious as God's salvation should be linked to something as menial as water-carrying. Yet God has always entrusted his kingdom-building work to those whom others might overlook.

If water is a sign of God's glorious, breakthrough presence, then Isaiah 12 shows us yet another means by which it touches our world. Sometimes it's a rolling sea; sometimes it's a river bringing a desert to life; and sometimes it's a well whose waters can be drawn by anyone and carried to whoever might need them.

Will you be a water-carrier today? Your bucket might be a word or a hug, a smile or an act of kindness, but if you do it prayerfully then you will have filled it full of the water of God's presence and it will refresh and revive.

Have there been water-carriers in your life lately – people who've given you a taste of God's goodness just when you've needed it? Give thanks for them today, and why not thank them in person next time you see them?

LYNDALL BYWATER

Asking for springs

[Aksah] replied, 'Do me a special favour. Since you have given me land in the Negev, give me also springs of water.' So Caleb gave her the upper and lower springs.' (NIV)

During the summer, our local Churches Together group received a request to make up welcome boxes for some families visiting Canterbury on holiday. The timescale was tight, so I emailed around the network, hoping we might at least gather enough to make a small gift for each family. Three days later, my front room was piled high with tea, coffee, cake and biscuits. I asked for the bare minimum and I got an abundance.

When it comes to prayer, Caleb's daughter Aksah is something of a hero of mine. Her father had given her some land as her marriage dowry, but the land he'd given her was desert, so it would be almost impossible to cultivate. She was left with a dilemma: should she just make do, getting the best use she could from it, or should she ask for a water source so that the land could be irrigated and farmed? She chose to ask, and if she'd had any doubts about whether it was the right course of action, they must have been dispelled by the generosity of her father's response. He didn't just give her one spring, he gave her two – the source and the overflow.

Now think about the story again, remembering that water is a symbol for God's tangible presence in our lives. Our Father in heaven is even more abundantly generous than Caleb was. He loves us to ask because he loves to give to us, and the thing he most loves to give us is his presence – not just enough, not just the bare minimum, but an abundance.

It may not be possible to change your circumstances, but you never have to just 'make do'. God delights when you ask for the springs of his presence to revive your desert places.

Loving Father God, thank you that you see the situations in my life that seem hopeless and dead. I come to you to ask for the water of your presence. Spring up and bring life to my desert places.

LYNDALL BYWATER

Digging ditches

And it came about while the musician played, that the hand (power) of the Lord came upon Elisha. He said, 'Thus says the Lord, "Make this valley (the Arabah) full of trenches."' (AMP)

I don't enjoy having to tell other people about the mistakes I've made in life. I prefer to get them sorted with God and then pack them away so that they don't tarnish my shiny image of myself. But as I listened to my friend tell her painful story, I knew that my pride would need to take a back seat, and that the next sentence out of my mouth would need to be: 'I've been there, done that and I know how it feels.'

The Israelites were dying of thirst, trapped in a battle they couldn't win. Through his prophet Elisha, God promised to rescue them and to fill the valley with pools of water; some translations read that he told them to dig ditches in the hard ground of the desert where they were fighting. Then he used something as simple and powerful as water to turn back their enemies. Difficult situations are no problem for God. We may have cornered ourselves in disastrous places, but if we will only get down on our knees and dig the ditches, God's presence can flow in and transform our battlefields to places of victory for ourselves and others.

What does it mean to dig ditches in our battlefields? For me, it means reflecting on what happened, repenting where I know I did wrong things and then letting God's love heal and restore me. It means spending time listening to him through his word and his Spirit so that I can learn to see myself the way he sees me, and it means praying for courage to live differently in the future. When we do those things, those places of failure get filled up and soaked through with his presence, and we can help others find grace and strength in their battlefields too.

Is there a situation that has left you with a lot of rubble – pain, shame and fear, perhaps? Take time to do some digging in prayer and reflection today, opening those broken places so that God's presence can flow in.

LYNDALL BYWATER

Detours and blockages

Now the Jordan is in flood all during harvest. Yet as soon as the priests who carried the ark reached the Jordan and their feet touched the water's edge, the water from upstream stopped flowing. (NIV)

If ever I find myself frustrated about how long it's taking to get somewhere, you can bet your bottom dollar that one of my ever-so-wise friends will utter the teeth-grindingly irritating phrase, 'It's all about the journey.' As one who likes to get from A to B as efficiently as possible and who finds detours profoundly irritating, I usually greet this cliché with a growl!

It's probably a good job, then, that I wasn't travelling with the Hebrew people when they escaped slavery in Egypt. After all, a journey that should have taken a matter of weeks took them 40 years, on a very circuitous route. You're probably familiar with the fact that their disobedience caused those decades of delay, but did you know that God deliberately diverted their route on two occasions so that they'd have to cross water? When they left Egypt, he chose not to lead them by the quickest route, because they'd meet enemies, so he led them via the Red Sea. Then, later, when they were ready to enter the promised land, instead of leading them in through the Negev desert, he brought them round to the Jordan River, which just happened to be in flood.

Did God just want to prove his power? That was certainly part of it, but since we're exploring the idea of water as a sign of his presence, perhaps we should look at these crossings from a different angle. By leading them to impassable bodies of water, it's as though he himself was blocking their way. They'd have to walk right into the water – into his awesome presence – to get where they needed to go.

God's intention is never simply to get us from A to B. His intention is always to bring us to himself.

We usually assume blockages happen because other people are being awkward or the enemy is at work. Think about the blockages you face at the moment. Could they be God's way of making his presence felt in your life?

LYNDALL BYWATER

At home on the water

But Jesus immediately said to them: 'Take courage! It is I. Don't be afraid.' (NIV)

Horatio Spafford was a lawyer in Chicago in the 19th century. He decided to travel with his family to Europe, but got delayed on business at the last moment, so sent his wife and four daughters on ahead of him. Their ship was sunk in a collision, and only his wife survived. As Spafford sailed across the Atlantic to join her, his ship passed near the place where hers had sunk, and in that moment of grief, he penned these words:

> When peace like a river attendeth my soul,
> When sorrows like sea billows roll,
> Whatever my lot, he has taught me to say,
> It is well, it is well with my soul.

Storms have a habit of making us feel like God is absent. The disciples must have felt that as they battled the wind and waves through that long Galilee night. Jesus had once calmed a storm for them, but this time they were on their own. Then the strangest thing happened. Their friend walked to them across the surface of the lake, as though he was strolling along the beach. He was completely at home on the water.

Water represents God's presence, but that presence is no guarantee of easy times. Sometimes it blocks our way, and sometimes it is a place of storms. The courage and comfort don't come from the absence of turmoil, but from the presence of the one who walks the very waves themselves. He is thoroughly at home in even the most raging of seas. If you're facing a storm today, it's not separating you from God. It is happening right in the midst of his presence, and if you put your trust in him, all will be well with your soul.

Eternal God, thank you that even though this storm may be scary, it is happening right in the midst of you. In the turbulence, may I know you beside me, holding me steady and lifting me up.

LYNDALL BYWATER

Raw material for blessing

Then [the master of the banquet] called the bridegroom aside and said, 'Everyone brings out the choice wine first and then the cheaper wine after the guests have had too much to drink; but you have saved the best till now.' (NIV)

I am part of a prayer community in Canterbury and we run a little drop-in shop. We open several afternoons a week, and each session finishes with a time of prayer. To our surprise, this 15-minute slot is one of the most popular things we do, particularly for those who come to us with no faith at all. We may make great tea, our company may be delightful and we may even be able to give good advice on things, but the bit they love most is the prayer. I think perhaps it's because that's when the 'tipping point' happens – that moment when God's presence breaks through in a more tangible way.

Today's story is one of the oddest miracles in the gospel accounts. Why on earth did Jesus feel the need to supply a wedding with vast quantities of excellent wine? It doesn't seem as worthy as a healing, does it?

This was the first miracle in Jesus' public ministry, and it involved water. Given our theme, this might not surprise you much anymore. As his friends and family watched him, he called up six huge jars of water – that symbol of God's glorious presence – and something wonderful quite literally flowed out of them. As a result, the wedding reached new heights of joyful celebration.

God's presence is the very best thing we have to offer anyone. It is the source of life, the antidote to brokenness and the primary agent in every miracle ever done in Jesus' name. When we 'fill up' on God's presence, wonderful things are released for those around us. That's why prayer is so important. When we pray, we stop trying to fix things and people ourselves, and we welcome the tangible presence of God to break in, bringing the very best.

If you make anyone a drink today, the chances are you'll use water. Before you hand it over, stop for a moment and pray. Invite God's presence to invade their lives as they drink. It might even turn to wine!

LYNDALL BYWATER

Mud and water

Then Jesus spat on the ground and made some clay with his saliva. Then he anointed the blind man's eyes with the clay. And he said to the blind man, 'Now go and wash the clay from your eyes in the ritual pool of Siloam.' (TPT)

I've been blind since birth, and for the most part I never have cause to seek medical treatment because my condition is stable, but about 14 years ago I had an accident that left me needing treatment from an ophthalmic consultant in London. My appointments always took twice as long as they should have, because my eyes are something of a medical rarity, so he would invite all the student doctors he could find to come and look at them!

I'm guessing the blind man in today's story knew what it felt like to be poked and prodded by a host of medicine men trying to cure his blindness, so when the Rabbi from Galilee put mud in his eyes and then told him to wash in a pool, he probably thought little of it. After all, why not try one more bizarre cure? And this one worked, but it didn't work because the mud was particularly rich in sight-restoring minerals, or because the water of Siloam had magical properties. It worked because two men's actions released the power of God's tangible, life-changing presence.

We're exploring the biblical image of water as a sign of God's glory – his breakthrough presence – but mud has a particular significance in scripture too. In the creation story, God made Adam from the dust, or mud, of the earth (Genesis 2:7), so mud signifies 'humanness'. Jesus put mud on the man's eyes, and it must have felt like a thoroughly human, thoroughly anti-climactic moment, because no healing came. Then the man chose to follow Jesus' advice and added water to the mud, and suddenly he could see.

Do you ever feel like your efforts are very ordinary? Be encouraged that when you ask God to draw near, his presence makes ordinary efforts into extraordinary miracles.

As you do the things life requires of you today, stop regularly in prayer, asking God to add his glorious presence to your human endeavours. He is with you always, but he loves to be welcomed in by your prayers.

LYNDALL BYWATER

Baptism

'I baptise you with water for repentance. But after me comes one who is more powerful than I, whose sandals I am not worthy to carry. He will baptise you with the Holy Spirit and fire.' (NIV)

I got baptised in my early 20s at the Anglican church I attended. Our baptistry was a coffin-shaped box, and you'd be lowered down to lie in the water on your back. The moment was glorious for all sorts of reasons, but the thing I remember most about it was the vicar putting his hand on my forehead and pushing my head under the water. When I joked afterwards that I wasn't sure he'd let me back up again, he replied: 'I just wanted to make sure you got a proper soaking.'

It has stuck with me because it says so much about what baptism is. John was at pains to explain to people that there was a difference between his baptism and the baptism Jesus would offer. John's was the repentance baptism – the one where you entered the water as a sign of being sorry and wanting to change. Jesus' baptism would be so much more. Jesus' baptism would mean a thorough soaking in the very presence of God, by his Holy Spirit. Perhaps that's why, when he asked John to baptise him, Jesus came up out of the water to find that the veil between earth and heaven had been lifted. The Spirit came, the Father spoke and for a few moments the Jordan River hosted the fullness of God's glory.

Being cleansed from the sin of our old life is of course still a vital part of baptism, but we miss out if we stop there. God doesn't want us just to get cleaned up; he wants to make us alive with himself. Whether you choose to get baptised as an outward testimony of your faith or not, never forget that God is always longing to give you a proper soaking in his glorious presence.

Next time you have a shower or bath, stop for a minute to notice what it feels like to be immersed in water. What does that experience tell you about the way God wants to immerse you in his presence?

LYNDALL BYWATER

Inundated

'Look! I am about to cover the earth with a flood that will destroy every living thing that breathes. Everything on earth will die.' (NLT)

Part of Jim Brazzil's job as prison chaplain in Texas was to attend executions. One of only two people allowed in the room, he would put his hand on the prisoner's leg as the lethal drug was administered. He said:

> I just want to be with the person one-on-one, not with any kind of agenda... I just want to bring them the peace of God.
> 'Watchman on the Walls', *Christianity Today*, May 2001

Almost two weeks ago, we read a prophecy about the awareness of God's glory covering the earth as the waters cover the sea. Today, we read a story about a flood covering the earth. Perhaps you think of these accounts as being many centuries apart, but in fact the flood story was probably written down a couple of centuries after Habakkuk's prophecy. Its authors would have known the prophecy and the traditional understanding that water was a symbol of God's presence.

We tend to think God withdraws when sin is around. We assume Noah's story is about God stepping away from his creation and unleashing the floodwaters as an agent of punishment and purification, but it changes when we remember that water signifies God's presence, not his absence. Sin breaks God's heart, but he doesn't need to avoid it for fear of contamination. Jesus died a death reserved for the worst of criminals because God's presence will always flow to the lowest place. It's not always easy: it may wash, purge or even destroy while it's there, but it will also redeem.

Jim Brazzil chose to draw near to those men and women who had committed terrible crimes, and it's a beautiful picture of God's heart. God longs to inundate even the darkest places with his refining, restoring presence.

Is there somewhere you know God is asking you to go – a place or situation where people's lives have been broken by sin? As a carrier of his presence, you can make a difference, just by being there and praying.

LYNDALL BYWATER

Living water

On the last and greatest day of the festival, Jesus stood and said in a loud voice, 'Let anyone who is thirsty come to me and drink. Whoever believes in me, as Scripture has said, rivers of living water will flow from within them.' (NIV)

I was in the café at Ikea on the day the Mayan Calendar said the world would end. My friends and I thought that would be a suitable location in which to witness the dismantling of all things, should the Mayan philosophy happen to be right in its predictions. It wasn't, but the meatballs were good.

On the final day of the Feast of Tabernacles, the priest would pour a jug of water into the basin next to the altar. It was a solemn ritual, full of symbolism, because it was a reminder that God's presence was right there, in that holy place. (After Wednesday's reading, you might find it interesting to know that the water was brought from the pool of Siloam, where the blind man washed his face.)

It was into this most holy of moments that Jesus spoke these words about living water. The atmosphere must have been electric, because what he was saying was utterly unheard of. He was saying that, instead of being found in a holy place, poured out by the hand of a priest, the living water of God's glory would flow through any human being who wanted it. The idea that 'ordinary people' could contain the very presence of God would have been unthinkable to Jesus' listeners.

Yet perhaps this is the answer to the riddle posed by Habakkuk in our very first reading almost two weeks ago. When millions of us human beings contain God's tangible presence, living lives which are so soaked in his living water that we can't help leaving puddles of it wherever we go, then the knowledge of the glory of God really will cover the earth, as the waters cover the sea. And whether I am in Ikea or not, that will be a breathtakingly beautiful day.

Before you move on from this theme, spend some time reflecting on what it means to you to be someone who carries God's presence – someone who bubbles over with his living water. How might that change the way you live?

LYNDALL BYWATER

Book 1 of the Psalms (1—41)

Helen Williams writes:

I've been watching red kites wheeling overhead today. Surveying the scene beneath them, taking in the big picture, they eventually dive down to pounce accurately on their prey. Over this next fortnight, we're going to do something like that with book 1 of the Psalms. Though tempted to just pick my favourites and ignore the more challenging psalms, I have felt compelled to take a bird's-eye view of all 41, frequently swooping down for a closer look at a theme, promise or challenge. I know I tread on holy ground, as these honest expressions of praise, wonder, anger and despair are personal to each of us and, for many of us, they have seen us through challenging seasons of our life.

I have given a little background information, while drawing out some recurring themes and pausing for prayer and reflection. I've suggested up to 30 verses to read each day, but sometimes these will make reading a bit disjointed, so I hope very much that that there will be times when you manage to read the whole of the psalms set. I know they will bless you.

As I was writing this week, I learnt of the death of the great soul singer Aretha Franklin. A mourner said of her music: 'Whatever you are going through, there's a song for you.' What could be a better description of Psalms? These are songs for both congregational and personal use and we know that Jesus knew, sang and often quoted them.

Amazingly, the earliest psalm in the collection of five books was written by Moses around 1410BC! The rest were written over a thousand-year period by several authors, of whom King David was the biggest contributor. The first book contains psalms exclusively of, about or for him, and they are still as fresh and relevant today as they were when he penned them.

The fourth-century patriarch, Athanasius, hit the nail on the head when he said that 'the rest of the Bible speaks *to* us, but the Psalms speak *for* us'. These songs help us give voice to our doubts, our pain and our frustrations as well as our gratitude, praise and worship. They are 'a school of prayer', wrote Eugene Peterson. They train us in how to respond to God and 'we don't learn the psalms until we are praying them'. May we draw closer to God this fortnight as we pray the Psalms together.

Delightful

Blessed is the one who does not walk in step with the wicked… but whose delight is in the law of the Lord, and who meditates on his law day and night. That person is like a tree planted by streams of water, which yields its fruit in season. (NIV)

Many of the chalk streams around where I live are home to watercress production sites. The clean, mineral-rich, flowing water provides just the right conditions for its flourishing. Needless to say, watercress soup is often on the menu here! Despite the unprecedented droughts we've seen across Europe, as I write the watercress is looking lush. The psalmist knew that those who delight in God's word are like the watercress, planted by (or even 'in') 'streams of water' (1:3).

Whenever I read these verses, I determine to live a more deeply rooted life, alive with fresh leaves and fruit of the Spirit, but it's not long before I uproot myself from the living water which flows so freely and then wonder why I feel so dry and dead. Slippage from God's purposes for us can be very subtle – first we might walk with the 'wicked', then stand with them, but before long we find ourselves sitting with 'mockers' (1:1). Let's get back to the one who provides living water and drink deeply.

The key to freshness is twofold – first, there's the decision not to keep step with those who reject God's ways, and second, a determination to root yourself in God's word. What does it mean to meditate on and even 'delight' in God's word (1:2)? This suggests lingering, reflecting, absorbing and enjoying. Is that your experience of reading the Bible? As we let God's words and promises in the Psalms soak into us, may we end up loving his words and wanting to linger.

Psalm 2 is about Solomon and is quoted throughout the New Testament. It points prophetically to another descendant of David, to a flawless King. This connected psalm ends where Psalm 1 begins – with the key to happiness: 'Blessed are all who take refuge in him' (2:12).

Choose a truth, promise or challenge from these two psalms and meditate on it through today, wherever you might find yourself. Ask God to help you 'delight' in what he shows you. May his living water refresh you.

HELEN WILLIAMS

Selah!

You, Lord, are a shield around me, my glory, the one who lifts my head high. I call out to the Lord, and he answers me from his holy mountain. I lie down and sleep; I wake again, because the Lord sustains me. (NIV)

Psalm 3 is the first prayer in the psalter and it's a heartfelt cry for help, expressing emotions we might all identify with. It was written towards the end of his life, when David is reaping the results of having indulged his son, Absalom, and is now running for his life (see 2 Samuel 15—18). Despite his distress, David is confident of deliverance. He remembers God's words to Abram in Genesis 15:1: 'I am your shield, your very great reward.' (The Hebrew word *magen* for 'shield' can also mean 'king'!)

I love the other picture he uses, which he probably took from a law court. He describes the action of a judge who lifts the accused from the ground as a sign of their acquittal: 'the One who lifts my head high' (3:3). Jesus has acquitted us, so let him pick you up; lift off your load; gently tilt your head to look into his eyes; and speak to you. The word *selah* is usually held to mean a pause for silence or an instrumental solo, space to focus on God's character. Have a *selah* moment now!

David ends this group of psalms in the same way he began, with confidence that the Lord is a shield for his people (5:12). As we pray the psalms, we find there are words here for fears we may be facing; threats to our wellbeing; questions we are wrestling with, and even disappointment with God. How important it is to cry to God honestly about what we're up against, and to cling, with David, to the truths we know – that he will sustain us, lift our head, shield us, hear us, give us peace and even bless us!

---

*A prayer for today: 'Lead me, Lord... make your way straight before me'
(Psalm 5:8).*

HELEN WILLIAMS

Amazing grace

Have mercy on me, Lord, for I am faint; heal me, Lord, for my bones are in agony. My soul is in deep anguish. How long, Lord, how long? Turn, Lord, and deliver me; save me because of your unfailing love. (NIV)

I once led a retreat in Winchester Cathedral for the leadership team of our church's women's group. One of the things we did that day was to climb the cold, hard, medieval Pilgrim Steps on our knees! It was a very palpable way of articulating our sorrow for past sin. Psalm 6 is the first of seven penitential psalms and finds David begging God to forgive his sin; weeping through the night; 'worn out' with his groaning – his couch 'drenched' with tears and his soul in 'deep anguish'. Here is someone who knows what it's like to experience failure, oppression and alienation, and here are words to help us express our deepest emotions.

Despite his deep anguish (6:1–7), David begins to remember God's faithfulness (6:8–10), and Psalm 7 shifts into a more confident mood, proclaiming that God will save and deliver (7:1), is the judge we can trust (7:11) and will bring evil to an end (7:9).

The phrase 'unfailing love' (6:4) is a translation of the Hebrew word meaning 'loving-kindness' or 'covenant mercy'. This powerful word occurs 127 times in Psalms and is the nearest Old Testament word we have to 'grace'. God loves us, is merciful, forgives us, eradicates our sin and sets us on the right path again. Thank you, Lord!

Although such a personal cry, Psalm 6 was intended for congregational singing (accompanied by strings). Psalm 7 is a *shiggaion* – a lyrical poem expressing strong emotions with appropriate music, and it's more of a personal lament over the disloyalty of one of Saul's courtiers, Cush the Benjamite.

'The Lord has heard my weeping. The Lord has heard my cry for mercy' (Psalm 6:8–9). Tell God how life is for you now and ask for his mercy. I know he will find ways to remind you of his grace.

HELEN WILLIAMS

Stargazing

When I consider your heavens, the work of your fingers, the moon and the stars, which you have set in place, what is [humankind] that you are mindful of them, human beings that you care for them? (NIV)

Last week, I was staying in a house on a hill in rural France – and when I say 'rural', I mean rural! The guests were people of faith and of no faith, but every evening, after dinner, we could not help ourselves stepping on to the terrace to sit or lie down and look at the vast dome of heaven above. With no light pollution, we could see more stars than you can possibly imagine: distant galaxies, planets and shooting stars. Every person there, in their own words, expressed something of what David writes here: 'What is [humankind] that you are mindful of them, human beings that you care for them?' (8:4). It was truly moving.

Of course, contemplating the miraculous star-studded sky puts things in perspective, making us and our concerns seem very small, but David reminds us that God has also designed us for glory and honour, giving us responsibility for everything he has made (8:5–6). Might this reminder make you see yourself differently today?

It's interesting that he speaks of the power of children's worship too (v. 2) – a theme Jesus picks up in the temple courts in Matthew 21:16. If you're in a position to be able to encourage any children in their faith, then rejoice in that but be prepared to learn from them too!

Psalm 9 begins with exuberant praise: David worships God 'with all [his] heart' (9:1) and, despite things being tough, the beginning of Psalm 10 reminds us to trust what we know of God, even when he may appear to be absent. I'm challenged by this discipline of worshipping God wholeheartedly, whatever the circumstances.

If you don't already keep a journal, it might be helpful to start one. Looking back at what you've written (however sporadically), seeing how God has led you, is faith-building. Take a selah *now and praise him with Psalm 8.*

HELEN WILLIAMS

Being the change

Who may live on your holy mountain? The one whose way of life is blameless, who does what is righteous, who speaks the truth from their heart; whose tongue utters no slander, who does no wrong to a neighbour, and casts no slur on others. (NIV)

Psalms 11—15 describe two ways to live, one for the 'wicked' and one for the 'blameless'. You can sense David's heartache over Israel, the country Samuel had built on godly foundations, now being eroded by the unfaithful Saul. In the first half of David's psalm-writing days, he was a fugitive, helplessly watching this happen; in the second half, he was able to play his part in rebuilding a God-led culture.

We may not come from a royal house or be a political leader, but we can hear, in David's heart-cries, principles for being the change in our own society. First, we must 'take refuge' in the Lord (11:1) and praise and acknowledge his lordship (11:4). Then we ask for his help (12:1) and trust his words (12:6). If he doesn't answer immediately, we must be tenacious (13:1). Placing ourselves at the heart of his love, we carry on worshipping and keep believing that he will act (13:5–7). Then we just get on with being blameless, righteous, truthful, trustworthy, consistent, generous, honourable, building up and honouring of others (15:2–5)! That's all!

What is God's reaction to this? He says: 'I will now arise… I will protect them' (12:5). Simple as that! These are the first actual words of God in the Psalms – what scholars call a direct 'oracle' and what David describes as the 'flawless' words of God, purified like silver and refined like gold.

We may feel hopeless about the developing culture around us, or we may despair of some of the political leadership across the world, but let's decide to trust the promises of God, celebrate his power and love, live faithful to him and pray for his kingdom values to begin to seep into every area of our personal, national and international life.

Today, let's get on our knees and pray for God's rule in our world. Ask his Holy Spirit to equip us to be the change wherever he has placed us.

HELEN WILLIAMS

Stirred not shaken

The boundary lines have fallen for me in pleasant places; surely I have a delightful inheritance. I will praise the Lord, who counsels me; even at night my heart instructs me. I keep my eyes always on the Lord. With him at my right hand, I shall not be shaken. (NIV)

A few years ago I was diagnosed with breast cancer. Praying this psalm was a profound help, especially in the days of not knowing, before surgery and a prognosis. All I needed to do was 'take refuge' (v. 1) in God and discover him to be 'my portion and my cup' (v. 5). I found he would often 'counsel' me and even 'instruct' my heart at night' (v. 7) as I lay awake, gripping a holding cross in my hand. I look back on that time gratefully for what I learnt about keeping my eyes 'always on the Lord' (v. 8) and trusting that he would 'make known to me the path of life' (v. 11). Whether I was to live or die, I knew I would know 'joy in [his] presence' (v. 11).

It may be that you are on a similar or much harder journey at the moment. Whatever you're going through, I pray you will 'not be shaken' (v. 8) and that your 'body will also rest secure' (v. 9). This is a more private, personal song than the previous psalms; may it be a reassuring song for you to sing to your heavenly father.

Verse 7 is a cry of trust in our ever-present teacher. Hebrew poets used to enhance the meaning and impact of ideas by 'paralleling them': repeating the same idea but in different words. Here, the statement about God being our counsellor is paralleled with the following statement about our heart being instructed, thereby underlining the importance of this precious truth.

One final personal response to this psalm: I have always found saying verse 6 out loud a challenge when feeling discontented! Praising God in the midst of troubling times inevitably changes our heart. It can be uncomfortable, but try it now.

Take time to read this psalm out loud and make it your personal prayer of confidence in God.

HELEN WILLIAMS

Say a little prayer

As for God, his way is perfect: the Lord's word is flawless; he shields all who take refuge in him. For who is God besides the Lord? And who is the Rock except our God? It is God who arms me with strength and keeps my way secure. (NIV)

Coming home this afternoon, I was listening to the radio in the car. They were playing one of Aretha Franklin's best-known songs, 'Say a little prayer'. Knowing I was returning to write on Psalms 17 (the first psalm entitled 'a prayer') and 18, I was struck by the words of her song that asked God to answer her prayer now and declared her love for the Lord.

'Turn your ear to me and hear my prayer' (v. 6), sings David, and woven through these psalms is that sense of intimacy between him and his maker: 'I love you, Lord' (18:1), 'Show me the wonders of your great love' (17:7), 'Keep me as the apple [the pupil] of your eye' (17:8) and 'He delighted in me' (18:19).

We know that Aretha's song was for someone who would inevitably let her down. David, however, is singing to his rock, fortress, deliverer and strength, to the one who would stop at nothing to save him.

If you have time, do read the whole of Psalm 18: you will see mountains shaking, heavens dividing, thunder, lightning, and land and sea devastated by a nostril blast! There is nothing God won't do to rescue you! 'He reached down from on high and took hold of me; he drew me out of deep waters' (18:16).

He doesn't only rescue, though, he empowers! He leads us to 'spacious' places (v. 19) via a 'broad path'; he turns our 'darkness into light'; and even enables us to face an army and 'scale a wall' (18:19–36)! Not only this, but he strengthens us, keeps our ways 'secure' and gives us secure footing like a deer, so that even the highest places are within our reach (18:32–33)!

Spend a moment remembering (perhaps even writing down) times when you've known God has rescued you. It's so easy to forget. Has he led you to a spacious place or turned your darkness into light? Praise him now.

HELEN WILLIAMS

World and word

The law of the Lord is perfect, refreshing the soul. The statutes of the Lord are trustworthy, making wise the simple. The precepts of the Lord are right, giving joy to the heart. The commands of the Lord are radiant, giving light to the eyes. (NIV)

Have you ever heard that great chorus from Haydn's 'The Creation'? 'The Heavens are telling the glory of God.' If you have, you'll probably start humming it now! It may not be your kind of music, but as a huge choir, soloists and instrumentalists weave lines of praise in and out of each other and crescendo to a powerful end, it offers an expression of wonder at how amazing our creator is. The words are based on the first few evocative verses of Psalm 19 and they are words that make me want to rush outside and marvel at his artistry. I would like to be attentive enough to hear the silent, yet richly articulate, voice of nature glorifying its maker.

His world speaks of God's reality and power, but we also need God's word, which speaks of his grace, his rules and his plan for our life. David extols all the attributes of God's word with awe and wonder. Notice all the description he uses in 19:7–14. More than this, look at what David finds through his study: refreshment, wisdom, joy, light and sweetness! This really makes me want to up my game and linger longer with God's word. I know he's always waiting to bless, but sometimes my devotions can be a bit perfunctory.

Psalm 20 is a different kind of song: it's generally thought to be the marching-into-battle anthem of the army of Israel. There is confidence in future victory here – it's in God's name, it's part of their past history and it's in the nature of the righteous judge. If this is the before-battle song, Psalm 21 is the after-battle one – the victory anthem, full of God's triumphs: 'We will sing and praise your might' (21:13)!

The word for victory in 20:6 is yeshuah, *the Hebrew name for Jesus. The Lord is victorious! Try whispering and proclaiming his name throughout today, and be on the lookout for the victories he will bring.*

HELEN WILLIAMS

The shepherd who became the sheep

My God, my God, why have you forsaken me? Why are you so far from saving me, so far from my cries of anguish?... They will proclaim his righteousness, declaring to a people yet unborn: He has done it! (NIV)

Last Sunday, my husband was preaching on Psalm 23 and I did some work on it with him, both of us aware that he had preached on it at hundreds of funerals over the years, but wanting its message to be fresh and powerful. What came out of our study was something you may have been aware of, but I had not: the fact that we really should read Psalms 22 and 23 together.

I have always been deeply comforted and reassured by the picture of the good shepherd, leading, protecting and refreshing. When my younger brother and my father died prematurely, I claimed his presence in the 'darkest valley' (23:4). I have looked forward to living 'in the house of the Lord forever' (23:6) too, but I find I have ignored the desperate cry of Psalm 22, Jesus' words on the cross: 'My God, my God, why have you forsaken me?' (22:1). Of course, I know that Jesus died for me, but I don't think I'd ever really internalised that he had to become the lost sheep in our place before he could become our good shepherd. What love for us, his beloved sheep!

Not only is he our shepherd, but Jesus is also the generous host. It's intriguing that he lays up the banquet table in the middle of the dark valley (23:5), not once we get out of it!

Psalm 22 reminds us of one of the scriptures Jesus cried from the cross (the other is in Psalm 31). On his way there, he had quoted Hosea, and you will remember his biblical retorts to Satan in the desert. We may try relaxation techniques, mindfulness and positive thinking, much of which can be useful, but in the end, the word of God is what sustains and inspires us.

'I am the good shepherd; I know my sheep and my sheep know me... I lay down my life for my sheep' (John 10:14–15). Read these psalms, perhaps aloud, and know you are in the good shepherd's loving gaze.

HELEN WILLIAMS

A sacred place

One thing I ask… that I may dwell in the house of the Lord all the days of my life, to gaze on the beauty of the Lord and to seek him in his temple. For in the day of trouble he will keep me safe in his dwelling. (NIV)

The five songs of Psalms 24—28 demonstrate a passion to spend time in God's presence. They come from different seasons of David's life but, from the exhortation in Psalm 26 to let the King of glory into both the tabernacle and into our heart, to the final verse of Psalm 28, with its cry that God would 'be their shepherd and carry [his people] forever' (28:9), they show David determined to be in relationship with him.

When he became king (c. 1000BC), David captured Jerusalem and brought the Ark of the Covenant to its rightful place in the city, where he built a new tent for it on Mount Zion. You can read about this in 1 Chronicles 15—16. On the day the tent (tabernacle) was dedicated, David offered sacrifices to God but commanded that no more blood should ever be shed there. This pointed prophetically to Jesus' once-for-all sacrifice. The tabernacle was designed with no inner room, as if to say that where God resides, there should be free access for all.

The Hebrew word used in Psalm 28:2 for the most holy place – *debir* – comes from the verb 'to speak'. We are reminded that, if we seek God's face (27:8), we will hear his voice and he will 'confide in those who fear him' (25:14) For David, the tabernacle was a place of refuge too: 'He will hide me in the shelter of his sacred tent' (27:5).

Is there a place where you go to encounter God alone? Over the years, I have set aside special places at home or gone to particular woods for time with God. Of course, he is not more present in these places than anywhere else, but maybe, in my anticipation, I make myself more present to him.

'I love the house where you live' (26:8), sings David. Find a place today where you can 'wait for the Lord, be strong and take heart' (27:14).

HELEN WILLIAMS

The splendour of holiness

Ascribe to the Lord the glory due to his name; worship the Lord in the splendour of his holiness. The voice of the Lord is over the waters; the God of glory thunders, the Lord thunders over the mighty waters. The voice of the Lord is powerful. (NIV)

'Britons are preparing for gale-force winds and torrential rain as Storm Ernesto looks set to crash into the UK,' my phone informed me. I smiled as I turned to Psalm 29 and read of the storm of God's presence. David's song carries us on a hurricane wind as God's awesome voice sweeps across the sea, down the whole length of Canaan and away into the desert, and, when the storm is finally spent, we see heaven opened and the Lord enthroned as King. Tremble before his majesty, David implies, and 'worship the Lord in the splendour of his holiness' (29:2). I'm reminded of the heaven-touches-earth scene in Isaiah 6, where the temple is full of God's holy glory and Isaiah is overwhelmed by his unworthiness.

Earlier psalms have given us models for intimacy with God. Here is something else entirely, and yet, despite the devastating effects of his glorious presence, almighty God gives his people peace – 'shalom' – a deep sense of wellbeing. As with Isaiah, who is cleansed and sent out as God's messenger, 'the Lord gives strength to his people' (29:11). After such an encounter, I want to say with Isaiah: 'Here am I; send me!'

Psalms 30 and 31 take us on in worship, and proclaim the privilege of being saved, healed, spared and made secure in God, our rock. We take comfort from David's testimony that joy always follows weeping.

Sometimes, the restoration of joy is about getting rid of the sin that separates us from God, and I have always loved Psalm 32 for its sound advice on healthy living: acknowledge what's gone wrong; allow God to forgive and restore you; hide away with him and wait for his instruction and counsel; and, above all, rejoice in his love.

Praise is 'inner health made audible', wrote C.S. Lewis. Is there anything inhibiting your worship today? Psalm 33 encourages us to sing 'a new song' to God. Maybe there's a new song of praise in your heart today?

HELEN WILLIAMS

The hiding place

I sought the Lord, and he answered me; he delivered me from all my fears. Those who look to him are radiant; their faces are never covered with shame… Taste and see that the Lord is good; blessed is the one who takes refuge in him. (NIV)

While on the run from Saul, David inexplicably left the comparative safety of the Judean desert to flee into Philistine territory (1 Samuel 21). He penned a cry for mercy (Psalm 56) after realising he'd made a terrible mistake! When God facilitated his 'mad' escape, David wrote this song of gratitude: Psalm 34. He wants his listeners, however tentative they might be about trusting God, to 'taste and see that the Lord is good' (34:8).

It's worth thinking about what taking 'refuge' (34:8, 22) in God means too. I imagine a child running to a parent for reassurance, burying their face and clinging tight while the adult calms, soothes and gently stands them on their feet again. The Hebrew word translated as 'radiant' (34:5) has the sense of an anxious mother's face lighting up when her lost child is found. There is something very powerful here about hiding in God and being found in him. What a change we might make if we were 'radiant' (like Moses in Exodus 34:29) after hiding with him.

Another crisis in David's colourful life gives rise to Psalm 35. Betrayed by both Absalom and Ahithophel, David curses his enemies in this 'imprecatory' psalm. Incidentally, both men died horrible deaths (2 Samuel 17—18). I confess I've often skipped over vindictive, revengeful psalms, embarrassed by psalmists' outbursts and calls for God's vengeance. I know there's much I don't yet understand about God's character. Paul quotes Deuteronomy 32:35 when he writes in Romans 12:18: 'Do not take revenge… but leave room for God's wrath, for it is written: "It is mine to avenge; I will repay."' Our screens are filled daily with people saying, 'I won't rest until I get justice!' Perhaps we can only fully forgive when we recognise and trust that God is the avenger.

'Taste and see that the Lord is good; blessed is the one who takes refuge in him' (34:8). Linger a moment with your heavenly Father today and listen to his heartbeat.

HELEN WILLIAMS

Let go and let God

How priceless is your unfailing love, O God! People take refuge in the shadow of your wings. They feast on the abundance of your house; you give them drink from your river of delights. For with you is the fountain of life; in your light we see light. (NIV)

I confess I much prefer to worship a 'New Testament' God of forgiveness and compassion, but secretly I wish I felt as strongly as David about those who turn their back on God to live a self-referencing life. Perhaps I would be a more effective evangelist if I took this more seriously.

Despite his opening outburst against the wicked in Psalm 36, it's not long before David is pouring out praise for God's righteousness, justice and saving love. This overflows into four beautiful metaphors: a refuge under God's wings; a feast of abundance; a river of delights; and a fountain of life (36:7–9). This beautiful and powerful poetry contains the heart of the gospel and these are verses to savour and internalise. 'In your light we see light' (36:9), he continues. The clarity and purity of God's presence scatters darkness and reveals truth. Let his light lighten your places of darkness or confusion today.

David writes Psalm 37 from the vantage point of old age and a life lived celebrating God's faithfulness, but he is still hoping that God will bring the wicked to justice. He reminds himself, and us, to leave vengeance to God: 'Be still before the Lord and wait patiently for him' (37:7). God's timing is rarely as we would like it to be, but so perfect! Three times David warns against 'fretting'. Fretting is such a common thing today – worry, resentment, jealousy, self-pity and anxiety all chew us up inside while accomplishing nothing. David's remedy is to 'trust in the Lord', 'do good', take delight' in him, enjoy your 'safe pasture', 'commit your way' to him and 'be still'.

If you feel confused or have been misunderstood, misrepresented or ignored recently, you will know this is really great advice: 'Let go and let God!'

'Take delight' in God today and spend some time praying these psalms. May you drink from the 'river of delights' and see the 'fountain of life' welling up in your life, overflowing into the lives of those you meet today.

HELEN WILLIAMS

The Lord who heals

I waited patiently for the Lord; he turned to me and heard my cry. He lifted me out of the slimy pit… He set my feet on a rock and gave me a firm place to stand. He put a new song in my mouth. (NIV)

If you're struggling with sadness or ill health at the moment, I hope David's words in today's psalms will help you express to God how hard you're finding life right now. Those assembling the psalter knew that honest lament before God is vital – pretence is not what he wants. Psalms 38—41 are designated for congregational singing too, which seems strange to us as we are not given to lamentation in our corporate worship. Perhaps we think we must protect God from what we feel? Of course, we know that a 'sacrifice of praise', when we're feeling low, restores godly perspective; but here is a model for corporate sorrow too.

Psalm 38 is another penitential psalm: David says, 'I am troubled by my sin' and begs for forgiveness, as well as listing the medical afflictions he's suffering with. This was probably written at the same time as Psalm 39, which is dedicated to Jeduthun, whose name means 'giving praise' – probably a nickname for Ethan, the worship leader!

David knows that God can heal: in Psalm 105, he reminds us that during the exodus from Egypt 'not one of them was sick'. He would have read in the Torah of 'Yahweh Rophek' (the Lord who heals), the healer of snakebites. He seems unembarrassed in all these psalms about continually nagging God for healing. The phrase 'waited patiently' (40:1) literally means 'waited-waited' in Hebrew!

Book 1 finishes with a final doxology of praise to God, as do all five books of the Psalms, stating that, whatever the psalmists have expressed of disillusionment, pain or distress in these songs, the overriding story is about God, and the final and undeniable glory and praise goes to him.

If you have time today, do look back over these last 14 days and ask God to bring to mind anything he has shown and taught you. Maybe even jot these things down but certainly pray them into your life.

HELEN WILLIAMS

Forgiveness and reconciliation: Philemon

Victoria Byrne writes:

This week's focus is Paul's brief letter to Philemon, in which he asks him to reconcile with a former slave, Onesimus, who ran away leaving a debt. This slave became a Christian through Paul, and is now his trusted colleague. This is a letter of reintroduction for Onesimus to carry to Philemon, reassuring him that this former runaway is now good news.

Who are the people mentioned in this letter? Paul, we know well. Decades after his humbling encounter with Jesus near Damascus, he is now a mentor and missionary who brought Philemon to faith. Timothy, we know especially from Paul's letters to him.

This letter tells us that Philemon, Apphia and Archippus co-lead their church. We know Apphia is a woman by the 'a' ending of her name. Paul was a former Pharisee, and women then had no social standing, yet Apphia was a co-leader in the church Paul planted. This shows the early church's radical attitude to women, which didn't match that of the world around them. Paul wants them to adopt a similar Christlike attitude to a former slave.

In the original Greek, the letter does not state that Onesimus was a slave, but his name means 'Profitable', which is the kind of thing slaves were called. 'Helpful' was another common name. Paul plays around with Onesimus' name, much of which is lost in translation. Reading commentaries on the text, I came to understand that Paul is writing to influence rather than dictate, so he makes use of implication rather than writing bluntly. If, like me, you hadn't studied this letter before, I would recommend exploring online resources or study Bibles. The thread of the letter is hard to track at first glance, but as it's only a page long it is well worth reading through slowly a few times before you dive in.

We don't know why Philemon and Onesimus fell out, which led to Onesimus running away. We do know that Christ restores his people into a body that would otherwise be broken and separated. This letter is a testimony to God's grace. He changes us from useless to valuable in his kingdom, just like Onesimus. As we shall see, reconciliation and transformation rely on forgiveness.

If you love them

I always thank my God as I remember you in my prayers, because I hear about your love for all his holy people and your faith in the Lord Jesus. (NIV)

I love talking to a Christian friend, Vera, who is in her 90s. We talked yesterday about the way long-term relationships survive difficulties and she told me about a poignant moment when she was visiting her husband in hospital a week before he died. They were holding hands and a nurse there asked them how long they had been married. '58 years,' said Vera, smiling. Rather surprisingly, the nurse's face fell. '58 years!' she said. 'How could you bear to be with only one person that long?' I asked Vera what on earth she had replied. She admitted she had been stunned, but blurted out, 'Well, if you love them, you want to be with them!'

That's what it all comes down to, isn't it? If we love someone, our willingness to remain in any relationship has to overcome threats of incomprehension, fear, anger and self-interest (and a hundred other temptations). Sometimes being loving and forgiving is an act of the will: we choose to respond to difficulties in a way that allows the relationship to continue and have a chance to improve. Often, the details of how that's ever going to happen are hidden from us at the time, but we choose to forgive anyway: to bless the other, to pray for them, to repent and persevere. We have faith in God, after all, that he wants to prosper us and will lead us through the valleys and out the other side. I can testify that he is willing and able to do that.

Paul starts his request to Philemon by affirming his loving habits and faith in Jesus, reminding him of the wider context of the work they shared together. Each of the concepts in verses 3 to 6 are rich points upon which to meditate.

How might these words from Paul (vv. 3–6) have impacted Philemon as he reread his letter and considered Paul's request?

VICTORIA BYRNE

Making relationships work

I pray that your partnership with us in the faith may be effective in deepening your understanding of every good thing we share for the sake of Christ. (NIV)

It sounds like Philemon plays a central role of some sort, officially or otherwise, among the Christians of his church. He clearly had good people skills. Does that mean Philemon had no trouble with the people around him? Was it easier among first-generation Christians? I don't think so. As someone who works in a church, I can testify that relationships always need work. Just look at the disciples' relationships, which sometimes degenerated into one-upmanship (Luke 9:46), jealousy and insecurity (John 21:21–22; Luke 10:38–42), and in the extreme, betrayal (see Judas).

Before asking Philemon to forgive an offence, Paul affirms Philemon's love for people and his Christian faith. Paul also wants the man's understanding of the gospel to deepen. Philemon's capacity for love, faith and gospel understanding will all grow if he forgives Onesimus. I recognise that's true for all of us, whenever we do it. As we do it, we will grow stronger. Forgiveness is always an act of will, often hard, whatever our position in life, however long we've been practising. The phrase 'practising Christian' is about right!

Sometimes, disagreement feels more painful when it's with Christians, because we're tempted to expect other believers to see things just as we do. When I feel like that, God reminds me of the value of each of his children, and that our diversity of perspective is a strength. As I become aware of wrong in myself as well, I find the humility to let their offence go, handing the 'right to judge' back to God. When I recognise my own faults, I become ever more thankful for God's patience in teaching me to love and forgive others and deepen my gospel understanding by applying it to my life.

Have you lost contact over time with someone you found hard to forgive? Is there anything that can be done?

VICTORIA BYRNE

Facing reunion, accepting change

Better than a slave, [he is] a dear brother. He is very dear to me but even dearer to you, both as a fellow man and as a brother in the Lord. So if you consider me a partner, welcome him as you would welcome me. (NIV)

Onesimus has run away and left debts: then he discovers God, through Paul, and becomes a changed man. Paul appeals to Philemon to let Onesimus return and be reconciled.

I'm aware that returning to a former environment as a changed person is a challenge. I'm travelling to a reunion with people I last saw eleven years ago. Even seeing my old stamping ground is poignant. I realise how much God has changed me and my situation since then, and also grown my faith.

How well God lets our past be our past! It says in Psalm 103, 'As far as the east is from the west: so far has he removed our transgressions from us.' I see a metaphor for distance, but also something else: east to west – 180 degrees! We cannot face in both directions at once: 'repent' means 'turn around'. Having turned to God, the place to which God has consigned our confessed sins is behind us in the opposite direction! Isn't that liberating?

Returning to an old environment can be hard. We are faced with the person we used to be. I wonder how Onesimus felt about seeing Philemon again. I imagine there would be joy at feeling the new strength, freedom and enlightenment of his present Christian outlook, in comparison with the person he was before. But one can fear feeling trapped into a past sense of self, especially when surrounded by people who only know the former you. At times like that, I make sure I go prepared: fully aware of how God sees me now. Perfect love casts out fear, and we are loved by God who knew us then, now and forever.

What fresh things does God have for you today? Ask him.

VICTORIA BYRNE

Forgiving and forgetting

I am sending him – who is my very heart – back to you... both as a fellow man and as a brother in the Lord. (NIV)

I live in Twickenham, where you will find, down by the riverside, a bench carved with quotations from the works of Alexander Pope, who lived a couple of streets away. One carving reads: 'Eternal sunshine of the spotless mind!', which I first came across as the title of a film. The film is an ode to the beauty of forgiveness in relationships. The characters see that they each fall short, forgive each other instead of 'running away' and (spoiler alert) give the relationship a future.

Urging forgiveness is not saying it's okay for someone repeatedly to be abusive and unloving towards you, while claiming to love you. Your safety matters to God: if you think something bad might be happening to you, consider contacting support charities in your location.

Moving on can mean letting go of something in the expectation of God offering something better in the future. Ironically, this summer I lost my phone by that inspiring bench, a phone full of journal entries and notes on what God had said during prayer over three years. It was a journal that I would reread to remember what God had done in my life. I went back to search for my phone, but someone must have taken it. Time, apparently, to move on.

A friend said to me recently, 'Forgiveness means reconciling oneself to the loss of not being paid back,' which helped me.

If Philemon is going to get help from a highly valued spiritual son (Onesimus) of his own spiritual father (Paul), he will have to forgive a big offence. In the process, he must recognise that Onesimus has become a new person, spotless in the sight of God. Not looking back, but pressing on.

Further study: Hebrews 12:1–3

VICTORIA BYRNE

Charge any costs to me

If he has done you any wrong or owes you anything, charge it to me.
(NIV)

Last week, I was struggling to arrange transport to a festival that I love attending. The simple solution was to hire a car, but God seemed to want me to travel with a friend who was still unsure of her plans. Though sincere in her offer, my friend had suggested sharing a journey with me once before and had to change plans at the last minute. To commit to travelling with her on this occasion felt risky, so I was uncertain what to do. Then one evening I felt God speak into my thoughts: 'Any costs, you can charge to me.' That was not something I would have come up with! I now realise he was quoting Philemon 1:18.

I contemplated the idea of God offering to bear my 'costs'. I found such grace and kindness in his generosity and reassurance. In that light, I was immediately ready to accept my friend's offer, as I felt sure that God was underwriting the 'risk'. In fact, the drive together was joyous and rekindled our friendship. God's words keep echoing in my mind. Doesn't he always bring a perspective that is higher and deeper, enabling us to see beyond the short-term loss or gain?

Paul is asking Philemon to forgive a real debt, and also urges him to forgive a relational debt, a breakdown in the relationship. Paul offers to cover the financial debt himself. I imagine the removal of that sense of outstanding debt removes a technical and emotional obstacle from Philemon's path to reconciliation and restitution, and helps the master to move forward with his former slave. God is not about patching things up and struggling on: he wants restitution and real forgiveness. That's what brings life.

Who is in spiritual debt to you today and how might God be calling you to reconciliation?

VICTORIA BYRNE

Restored relationships

Perhaps the reason he was separated from you for a little while was that you might have him back forever – no longer as a slave, but better than a slave, as a dear brother. (NIV)

Paul describes his vision for a restored relationship between Onesimus on the one hand and Philemon and his fellow house-church leaders Apphia and Archippus on the other. One commentator suggests that this reconciliation must have happened, or the letter would not have survived. If it had been destroyed right away, in fury, we would indeed not know of it!

What makes you overlook others' faults? When we really like someone, that helps us to overlook their faults. It's harder when we don't like someone! Some relationships present more challenges than others. I've come to realise that God equips us to fight for and nurture those relationships that he wants to strengthen and bless and that will bring glory to his name.

I once knew someone who regularly confided in me, but I felt what he was telling me was 'gossipy': I feared he undermined my trust in people I depended on. It made me not want to talk with him and maintain the relationship. However, I slowly started to see that he wasn't gossiping; he was raising questions because he was genuinely trying to fix things and he wanted to hear my different viewpoint. It took God to show me that.

It can be hard to decide if someone is sharing information for the right reasons. Some people may gossip out of insecurity, and that's a different problem entirely. That one I find more challenging! In hindsight, the real source of that challenge is the enemy: he doesn't want us to grow healthy and mutually supportive relationships. Gossip disguised as 'sharing' is insidiously destructive.

Maybe a relationship is particularly challenging because the enemy is opposing what God has strategically placed in your life. Asking God about his purpose for a relationship can lead us to fresh vision and hope.

Ask God which relationship he wants to talk to you about today, to give you a fresh vision.

VICTORIA BYRNE

Just okay or better than that?

Paul… and Timothy our brother, To Philemon… also to Apphia our sister and Archippus our fellow soldier – and to the church that meets in your home. (NIV)

While wondering what caused the breakdown of Onesimus' relationship with Philemon, I remembered that Paul had himself experienced a split with a colleague with whom he was later reconciled. Mark (the gospel writer), who is called John Mark in some instances, worked with Paul (Acts 12:25) and fell out with him (Acts 15:36–40) but they had reconciled by the time this letter was written (Philemon 1:24; Colossians 4:10; 2 Timothy 4:11). Those were some dramatic break-ups!

I'm about to attend another reunion, this time of people I knew as a teenager. I'm mildly anxious about seeing some of them again. There is no major wrongdoing to forgive but, since I'm writing this, I ask myself if any forgiveness is required, and I take the space to look to God for an answer. Mostly what I find in that space is the shyness I used to feel – anxiety that emanated from me, not chiefly from anything my friends did, and which limited my relationships.

I'm sure God wants even 'okay' relationships to be better than that. Do we want to accept mediocre relationships? Do we let small offences stop us knowing someone better? Years later, will we feel that someone would have been a great friend, had we only realised we had so much in common and worked harder on the relationship? Is repentance needed as well as forgiveness? We need God's grace to lead us into forgiving even small things, or else we may drag a bundle of offence along with us as we hold onto little resentments that limit and damage what could be wonderful relationships.

Not everyone is going to be a best friend. But if I commit to keeping short accounts with people and stay current with God, I will build healthy and God-honouring relationships. Further meditation: Hebrews 12:15.

VICTORIA BYRNE

Ruth's story: whispers of calling and grace

Hannah Fytche writes:

The beautiful story of Ruth begins with five painful verses. Naomi, we learn, fled with her family to Moab when famine threatened her hometown. Having lived in Moab for time enough to celebrate the weddings of her two sons, Naomi becomes a childless widow: her husband and sons die, leaving her with two daughters-in-law, Orpah and Ruth: lone women in a man's world; grieving widows, with no child to give their family hope.

Imagine you're with them as they weep and wonder. Naomi grieves for her homeland: she came to Moab to find food and life, but has lost everything. Where can she go next? How will she live? Ruth and Orpah married into a family with just two sons; there were no more sons that they could marry to continue the family line, as was the custom. Will they go home to their families? The first five verses of Ruth portray a desperate, sad situation. We weep and wonder.

Yet there is hope – there always is when God writes the story. Ruth's four chapters of quiet glory, nestled between Judges and the Samuels, whisper of the restorative generosity and kindness of God. As we read this story, we'll glimpse shining moments of God's glorious grace, a grace that transforms emptiness to fullness, bitterness to joy, foreignness to belonging, and the ordinary to the extraordinary. This is a grace that takes human lives, struggles and decisions, and calls them into a greater story.

We'll perceive deep truth, truth captured in an ancient Hebrew story and passed down through millennia to be in our hands. Consider this: Ruth's story was written in an ancient culture so different from our own, for purposes that we cannot certainly determine, yet it still speaks to us of the risk and reward of following God, the kindness and welcome he offers to strangers, and his steady and glorious character that we can trust completely. It still speaks of hope in the midst of sorrow and tough obedience that yields new life.

So let's pray, as we begin, for God to write these truths on our hearts. Let's pray for him to awaken our imaginations to the characters of Ruth's story and the possibilities that they inspire. Let's pray for him to give us courage to hear and follow his voice – into scripture, into transformation and into following him.

On the strength of a whisper

When Naomi heard in Moab that the Lord had come to the aid of his people by providing food for them, she and her daughters-in-law prepared to return home from there. (NIV)

Naomi, Ruth and Orpah: they stand close, and they weep and wonder. Where next? In their grief, they search for hope and direction – and they hear a whisper, a rumour: God was helping his people. The famine was ending. Naomi's home was becoming safe again.

They make preparations and begin the journey. On the strength of a whisper from God, they leave Moab, which is Ruth and Orpah's home and a place of loss and failed hope for Naomi. Mixed feelings would certainly have accompanied this trio of travellers.

Life is often a mixture of feelings. We're carried along by our calendar days, completing the tasks required to keep us going as well as responding to bigger events that punctuate our routines. These encounters can cause feelings of both joy and stress, happiness and sorrow, laughter and grief. Take a moment to consider how you feel, in this moment. What is happening in your life? What decisions are you making, or will you make today and this week? Are you going through a busy time socially or at work, or are your days quite restful? Are you, like Naomi, Ruth and Orpah, facing a heart-wrenching change because of loss, pain or something beyond your control?

Life really is a mixture. We can often feel a little lost, left searching for the right direction in the midst of both joy and sorrow. Learning to hold steady and walk in faith can be a challenge when things are busy, or changeful, or really exciting and joyful.

In the midst of this, Naomi found direction in a whisper: a rumour of God's faithfulness. It orientated her, gave her direction. On the strength of a whisper from God, she found the strength to keep going, even in the intensity of the events of her life.

Be still and listen. What is God whispering to you, in the midst of your everyday?

HANNAH FYTCHE

Courageous and compelled

But Ruth replied, 'Don't urge me to leave you or to turn back from you. Where you go I will go, and where you stay I will stay. Your people will be my people and your God my God.' (NIV)

On their journey back to Naomi's homeland, the three travellers reach a crossroads. Naomi urges Ruth and Orpah to return to their families; there is no hope of new husbands for them within her family. They should return home, find another husband and a new life. She would continue alone.

Orpah and Ruth wept, wondered and decided. Orpah kissed Naomi goodbye. Ruth clung tight to her mother-in-law: 'Where you go I will go.'

This is striking. Ruth chooses to stay with Naomi and make the ten-day journey back to Bethlehem. She chooses the long road with an uncertain end: as a Moabite, there was every possibility that she would not be accepted into Israelite society. Not only would she be a widow, but she would be a foreigner. Instead of going back to the safety of her home, Ruth chooses the long road and the risk.

Such tough courage must have a reason – a good one. Why would Ruth choose this? Was it because she loved her mother-in-law? Or because she had a reason for not returning home?

Maybe it's both of these and something more, something so compelling that Ruth *has* to follow. Naomi found the strength to journey home. Maybe that same whisper was compelling Ruth, catching her attention. Maybe Naomi's God, the God of the Israelites, was speaking to Ruth, the Moabite. Maybe something new was happening for Ruth: the God she'd only heard of in whispers was inviting her to follow him, reassuring her that all would be well.

We too can hear these compelling whispers and words of God. God invites each of us to new places as we follow him – new situations, relationships, jobs, risks, adventures. Take heart and follow him: where is he calling you to go?

Father, thank you that you compel your people to follow you courageously. Help me to listen to your voice and hear with a trusting heart where you want me to go – even if that place is new to me.

HANNAH FYTCHE

A stranger welcomed

At this, she bowed down with her face to the ground. She asked him, 'Why have I found such favour in your eyes that you notice me – a foreigner?' (NIV)

Ruth risks all, and follows a whisper into a new land. Here, she faces new challenges: she and Naomi are widows with no livelihoods. 'Let me go to the fields,' she petitions Naomi. She goes, and gleans grain behind the workers. I've never gleaned grain, but I reckon it's hard work, backbreaking under a blazing sun. Ruth chooses the long road, the costly action.

It was particularly costly as women working alone in fields were in danger of abuse by the men also working the fields. Ruth knew no one; she was without protection – or so she thought.

Before we read of Ruth gleaning grain, the narrator tells us a secret: 'Naomi had a relative on her husband's side… whose name was Boaz' (v. 1). With us knowing this fact, Ruth goes out to the field and a few sentences later the narrator puts in a humorous, important aside: 'As it turned out, she was working in a field belonging to Boaz' (v. 3).

Ruth was safe. From verse 8 onwards, we see Boaz's generosity towards Ruth, letting her work in his fields with protection, provision and extra grain left out for her (2:16). Boaz is extravagantly kind: he notices her, 'a foreigner', and gives her everything she needs. In place of emptiness and loss there is fullness, provided by the timing and grace of God at work in Boaz's generosity.

We can learn from this kindness. When a stranger wanders in, we can be people of extravagant welcome and kindness, guided by God's love. Ruth, a foreigner, was welcomed by an Israelite – and this was no small thing. A thread running through Ruth's story is that God welcomes her, a non-Israelite, a person not perceived to be his own. Who do we exclude? How can we notice, welcome and include them in God's love?

God, thank you that you are kind towards all people, calling all your own. You protected Ruth and prepared a welcome for her in a new place. Show me how to do the same for all who need it.

HANNAH FYTCHE

Under God's wings

'May the Lord repay you for what you have done. May you be richly rewarded by the Lord, the God of Israel, under whose wings you have come to take refuge.' (NIV)

In their first recorded conversation, Boaz speaks this blessing over Ruth. We've noticed how glimmers of God's grace shine quietly and gloriously throughout Ruth's story; here, we see a shining proclamation of God's character.

Boaz includes Ruth the Moabite in the Israelite God's rich blessing, demonstrating that God's love is inclusive. We see this throughout the narrative of the Bible: a widening of God's kingdom so that it includes *all* people. This brilliant truth is captured in Ruth's story in a very personal, individual context: the specific inclusion of one person, Ruth, as she follows God courageously.

Not only do we see this startling truth, but we also are given the gift of this beautiful phrase: 'under whose wings you have come to take refuge' (v. 12).

When I was younger, this phrase caught my imagination and provided comfort for me through many tricky moments. I started drawing a little symbol of God's wings curved over me (I was drawn as a little red dot) on my diary, my mirror, my hand, in books and notebooks. That drawing, from this verse, became a kind of prayer for me: a prayer that led me into the affirming presence of God, under whose wings I had taken refuge.

God is our safe space, our comforter and refuge in the midst of all else. Even while life swirls on around us, we can withdraw to that secret place and take refuge, as Ruth did, in the presence of God.

There are very practical ways we can do this. Pray, in whatever way is comfortable – go for a walk, write down what's on your mind, draw a little symbol of being under God's wings. Pray with people, too. God loves to make the church a place of refuge for his people.

Thank you, God, that whatever is happening, I can take refuge under your wings. You give me life and safety. Show me how to come to you for refuge. May I speak this blessing of refuge and love over others.

HANNAH FYTCHE

Known by name and not forgotten

'Don't call me Naomi,' she told them. 'Call me Mara, because the Almighty has made my life very bitter.'… 'The Lord bless him!' Naomi said to her daughter-in-law. 'He has not stopped showing kindness to the living and the dead.' (NIV)

Let's rewind to the start. Naomi has lost her husband and sons; she lives with the heavy weight of grief. Death tears an irreparable hole, and for Naomi it's worse: she will be returning to her homeland without those she loves, and will have to break the news to old neighbours.

She arrives in Bethlehem, with Ruth. Familiar faces think they recognise her: 'Is this Naomi [whose name means 'pleasantness']?' they ask. Naomi's eyes glisten with sharp pain. She is not the Naomi they remember; her life has not been pleasant. Her name no longer fits her. 'Call me Mara, ['bitterness'],' she replies. Naomi's life had become characterised by grief, pain and emptiness. 'The Almighty has afflicted me,' she cries. He has forsaken me; he has forgotten my name.

In life's bitter moments, you can feel you don't fit: you're all sharp edges and jagged words, because the wounds you're carrying run too deep. God can feel distant: an afflicter rather than a comforter, a colluder in causing you pain rather than the one who's binding your injuries.

Let's fast-forward. Ruth has been gleaning in Boaz's field, and comes to Naomi with extra grain and a story of great generosity. Naomi exclaims: 'Boaz is our close relative, one of our guardian-redeemers!' Her heavy heart, beginning to heal now she's in her homeland, is buoyed with joy. '[God] has not stopped showing kindness to the living and the dead.'

Naomi rediscovers God's faithfulness. She realises that God's kindness has been constantly there – something which the narrator hints at by never calling her 'Mara', but always 'Naomi'. Naomi has always been Naomi: God has always known her name and has never once forgotten her.

God, you know my name. Through every sorrow and joy you have not forgotten me. May I remember your kindnesses, that I might hold on to them and know that you do not forsake those you have made your own.

HANNAH FYTCHE

Practically there

When Ruth came to her mother-in-law, Naomi asked, 'How did it go, my daughter?' Then she told her everything Boaz had done for her and added, 'He gave me these six measures of barley, saying, "Don't go back to your mother-in-law empty-handed."' (NIV)

Boaz, Naomi revealed, is a 'guardian-redeemer' (2:20). A guardian-redeemer was obliged to care for relatives in difficulty. They could also marry the widows of their relatives in order to continue the family line, if there were no sons alive to fulfil this duty. This was important: land and status were inherited and preserved through bloodline.

This information illuminates Ruth 3 and 4, which narrates how Ruth and Boaz were married. Ruth and Naomi had the problem of Naomi's husband Elimelek's land – who would care for and inherit it?

Boaz was Naomi's answer to this problem. He was a guardian-redeemer, and he was kind. Naomi pragmatically suggests that Ruth should marry Boaz. This, after a chaste night on the threshing floor and a meeting at the town gate, is what happens. Ruth and Boaz marry. Elimelek's name does not disappear. There is great joy for Ruth and Naomi.

Naomi's pragmatism stands out. 'How did it go, my daughter?' Did our plan work as hoped? Will Boaz take care of us? Naomi is careful to anticipate the needs of her family – earlier, even in her grief, we saw her considering what would be best for her daughters-in-law (1:6–18).

God works in Naomi's pragmatism. Being practical is not mutually exclusive to being spiritual (a mistake we sometimes make). Naomi decides, she acts, and she sees God bringing fruit through her actions. Ruth goes to Boaz; God works in the details to see them married. God is seen again in Boaz's practical generosity: Boaz sends Ruth home from the threshing floor with barley, so that Naomi is not left 'empty-handed'. She has more than enough food.

Let us not forsake the pragmatic in favour of the spiritual. Let us anticipate our and others' needs and meet them when we can.

How can you practically serve someone today? Father, thank you that you've given us the ability to be pragmatic: to perceive need and rise to meet it. From our prayers bring action, and from our actions bring fruit.

HANNAH FYTCHE

On the strength of a whisper followed

This is the family tree of Perez: Perez had Hezron, Hezron had Ram, Ram had Amminadab, Amminadab had Nahshon, Nahshon had Salmon, Salmon had Boaz, Boaz had Obed, Obed had Jesse, and Jesse had David. (MSG)

Having married Boaz, Ruth gives birth to a son. More joy for Ruth and Naomi! Their lives have been transformed from grief to hope.

Their story concludes with a rather incongruous genealogy, yet I think it's a wonderful ending to Ruth's quiet story. It shines with glory.

It shines because it shows how this little tale, tucked away in the Old Testament, fits into the grand sweep of the biblical narrative. Ruth's son was Obed, named as of Perez's line. Perez's great-great-grandfather was Abraham, the father of nations. Obed's grandson was David, the great king of the Old Testament – and the one from whom the Messiah, Jesus, would be descended.

Turn to Matthew 1. Slipped in among the lines of that long genealogy is Ruth's name: 'Boaz the father of Obed, whose mother was Ruth.' Quiet Ruth, who risked all on the strength of a compelling whisper from God, is named in the opening verses of the gospel about Jesus Christ. Would she ever have imagined such a grace upon grace? She's one of only four women mentioned in Jesus' genealogy – there's Tamar, who had a child by her father-in-law; Rahab, the prostitute; Ruth, the Moabite; and Mary, the pregnant and unmarried teenager. It's striking and beautiful. It's the story of one widow printed into God's word and remembered for millennia.

You see, it's an example of the fruit God brings from our obedience and willingness to follow. God's whisper compels us to follow; our obedience, often as fragile as the flap of a butterfly's wing, amplifies that whisper to a roar. This is the life we're called to: a life of following a God who is deeply interested in our individual lives, and who weaves us into the living and extraordinary story of Christ. Ruth followed. Will you?

Think back to the first day we looked at Ruth. What was God whispering to you then? What has he been whispering to you since? Father, give me courage to follow. I know you will bring fruit.

HANNAH FYTCHE

The promise

Selina Stone writes:

Of all the stories in the Bible, the account of the birth of Jesus is probably one that most people think they know pretty well. Whether Christians or people of other faiths or none, our imaginations have been captured by the tale of the little baby born to a virgin in a stable because there was no room in the inn. Yet, when we look into this story with patient attention, we find that it has much more to offer us than fuzzy feelings or good material for church creatives. It is more than just a story of a little family from a long time ago or a moral lesson about a really well-behaved young woman whom God particularly liked. The story of the birth of Jesus is the story of the fulfilment of the promise made by God to his people. The Christmas story represents the moment when God acts in human history in a mysterious and unexpected way, changing the course of humanity forever.

In this series of reflections, we will be exploring the story of Jesus' birth as it is recorded in the gospel of Luke and the book of the prophet Isaiah. We will be peeling back the layers of the ancient prophecies to consider what God had promised to his people and what the coming Messiah would be like. We will also take our time to explore some of the different elements of the story of the birth of Jesus in the New Testament, and what it looked like when the long-awaited promised Messiah arrived in flesh.

For each of us on this journey of faith, we can identify both with the desire for a promise to be fulfilled and with the need for God's intervention. As people with our own limitations, we consistently need God to act in ways that we are not able to. We also have an inherent need for hope, which is where promises and fulfilment are so significant. My prayer is that as you journey through the passages and reflections over the next week and a half, you would be encouraged to believe more deeply in the God we meet in Christ, who intervenes in human experience in order to fulfil his promises.

Preparing for the promise

'And you, child, will be called the prophet of the Most High; for you will go before the Lord to prepare his ways, to give knowledge of salvation to his people in the forgiveness of their sins.' (ESV)

We all know what it feels like to anticipate the arrival of something new. Being the geek that I am, I particularly love the arrival of new books to my house. As soon as I have ordered them, I begin wondering where I will make room to put them on my categorised book shelf (yes, I am that bad). I have seen my friends prepare for the arrival of their babies by making room in their homes, buying new clothes, thinking of names. Preparation is a core part of getting ready to receive what you are waiting for; it is in itself an act of faith.

In this passage today, Zechariah, the father of John the Baptist, speaks prophetically about the son who has been given miraculously to him and Elizabeth in their old age. This baby has a special mission as a prophet who will be the forerunner for Jesus, 'preparing his ways'. Israel had been waiting centuries for this Messiah, there are around 400 years of history between the last word of the Old Testament and these narratives about the birth of Jesus. God, in effect, has to jolt them awake! He sends John ahead to encourage the people to make room and to rearrange their hearts through repentance so they can be ready to receive him. Even God-in-flesh does not choose to serve in isolation, but desires others to work alongside him in his work of salvation. John begins to prepare the hearts of the people and to point to Christ, to make sure nobody misses him when he arrives. John's ministry is one of glorifying Jesus and making sure he is known.

As you enter into this season of reflection on the coming of Jesus, the promised Messiah, how do you need to prepare your heart? Lay before him the struggles of this year. Prepare, in your own heart, a way for the Lord.

SELINA STONE

Faith in the promise

'And blessed is she who believed that there would be a fulfilment of what was spoken to her from the Lord.' (ESV)

Imagine yourself in the house of Elizabeth the day that Mary arrived. With no prior notice (with no texts or phones available), Mary arrives out of the blue at the house of her relative, who has been in hiding for five months since she became miraculously pregnant in her old age. As soon as Mary enters the house and greets her, Elizabeth's unborn baby leaps and she prophesies before Mary even gets a chance to tell her that she is pregnant with the Messiah. This is a girls' catch-up of historic proportions! (I like to think Zechariah was out chopping wood with his friends somewhere and left the women to share this moment…)

Elizabeth commends Mary for her faith in believing that the impossible was possible. There is no doubt in Elizabeth's mind (as she has also experienced this miracle) that this is God's doing. Can you imagine how powerful this moment is for Mary, who is affirmed by this older female relative? Mary had experienced so much turmoil in her relationship with Joseph, and we can imagine what she would have faced from her family and other members of her community. Yet here, Elizabeth commends Mary for her costly obedience.

These words of Elizabeth to Mary transcend time to touch our own hearts. There is a blessing available when we believe the word of God – it is not just the blessing of having what we hope for (which may not always come) but the blessing of offering to God the love and trust that he has given to us. It is the blessing of peace that the process and the outcome rest in his hands, not our own. It is the blessing of being simple as a child, standing under the gaze of our loving Father.

Heavenly Father, we can find it so difficult to believe your word, even when it comes so clearly to us. Please help our unbelief. Allow us to encourage others, and to develop relationships that will help us grow in faith.

SELINA STONE

The promise of the impossible

Mary said to the angel, 'How will this be, since I am a virgin?' And the angel answered her... 'Your relative Elizabeth in her old age has also conceived a son, and this is the sixth month with her who was called barren. For nothing will be impossible with God.' (ESV)

There are many people in the scriptures who, when hearing the call of God, ask, 'But how will this be…?' Out of all of them, this seems to be one of the most crucial because what the angel is telling Mary is not just unusual, it is, humanly speaking, impossible. Mary does not pretend she gets it. She is open with the fact that she does not understand, and she trusts God enough to ask – which, for me, is a marker of a life of faith. Faith and uncertainty work hand in hand; when we are unsure and doubtful, then we have the chance to truly exercise faith. If everything makes sense logically, and we can clearly see the path, then to follow is not faith; it is simply common sense. Mary models the kind of faith that only appears in situations of the impossible.

I find Mary's honest question very encouraging as I have often found myself wondering how God's words would transform my own life. I have had many moments of questioning, some that have been in the darkest moments of my life where I have asked God 'How?' and 'Why?' Instead of hiding away from God when we are unsure (which can seem like the natural response), God desires us to come near to him with all of our questions and to confess them. Like the angel pointing to Elizabeth, I often gain courage from hearing what God has done in the lives of others or remembering how I have experienced God at work in my life before. It builds our faith when we remember that God will always be true to his character and his purpose: to love us and to form the image of Christ within us.

What would it look like to build your faith in an area where you are struggling? Is there a book, a podcast or a person whose story could encourage you to expect what may seem impossible?

SELINA STONE

The promise fulfilled

For to us a child is born, to us a son is given; and the government shall be upon his shoulder, and his name shall be called Wonderful Counsellor, Mighty God, Everlasting Father, Prince of Peace. Of the increase of his government and of peace there will be no end. (ESV)

I am not sure what people said about you when you were born, or what you may have seen in the faces of the babies in your family. Being born into a Christian family, and a Pentecostal one at that, child dedications were always very significant moments in our church's life. Our pastor would pray for a child, and wait on the Holy Spirit for specific words, images or scriptures to affirm what God may be saying about the child and his or her family. They were always such special moments.

Today marks the great miracle of human history: when God became a man. These words in Isaiah came before Jesus was born, and are a prophetic declaration about this baby whose birth we celebrate today. They go way beyond the usual descriptions. Jesus is not prophesied to be a 'good' baby, or someone who will be smart or popular. There is no emphasis on whether he will be cute or good looking when he grows up... for *this* baby, the words of God are of profound and eternal significance.

Above all, he is born unto 'us' – not just to his parents and his family, but to us as a human family, across centuries and continents. This child has come for our sake on a mission of salvation for all creation. Under the inspiration of the Spirit, the prophecy declares that this child who is born will lay a foundation for the government of God. He will be known to us by his astounding wisdom, his powerful divinity, his loving fatherhood that never ends and the peace that is manifested in his presence. The good news is that this will not only be for a short time, but for eternity.

Christ is known to us in so many ways. As you spend time enjoying today with friends or family or having relaxing time to yourself, ask God to make himself known to you in the way you need him during this season.

SELINA STONE

Hope that sustains

And they went with haste and found Mary and Joseph, and the baby lying in a manger. And when they saw it, they made known the saying that had been told them concerning this child… Mary treasured up all these things, pondering them in her heart. (ESV)

The shepherds are amazed that they, a group of scruffy-looking (and probably smelly) guys in a field, have somehow been put on the list of VIPs to be informed by angels of the birth of the Messiah. This must have been the highlight of their lives and they waste no time in rushing to see what is going on. Mary, who is living through the most extraordinary experiences of her young life, finds herself surrounded by these shepherds, telling her all about angels singing a message from heaven about her baby son. It is too much for us, let alone Mary, to get our heads around. The scriptures record that she treasures up these things and ponders them in her heart.

I tend to keep hold of many things. Unfortunately, they are not always positive. I have a habit of 'treasuring up' or giving huge value to my failures, fears about the future or my insecurities. I can spend a lot of time pondering them, sometimes to the point of great anxiety. But Mary treasures up *these* things: these moments of amazement and awe when God has broken through so incredibly that even complete strangers come to see. She keeps hold of her joy and she ponders the mystery of God's faithfulness. She allows these wonderful things that are happening to build up a store in her heart, that she will no doubt need to draw on in future. Notice that she does not open 'these things' up to discussion, critique and evaluation – she keeps them safe from any discouraging or cynical voices. She helps us to see that while it is normal for us to want to share with others, it is also important that we discern when to reflect in quietness with God alone.

Take a moment now to reflect on your need to treasure and ponder as Mary did. Let us empty our hearts and minds of worry and fear, hopelessness and timidity, so that we make room to treasure faith, love, hope and joy.

SELINA STONE

Hope in the darkness

The people who walked in darkness have seen a great light; those who dwelt in a land of deep darkness, on them has light shone. (ESV)

You only need to have stubbed your toe when creeping around your bedroom at night to know how inconvenient darkness is when you are trying to get around. I enjoy sleep, and if I ever have to get up during the night, I will try to do it in the dark so the light doesn't wake my brain up too much and prevent me getting back to sleep easily. It works pretty well, except when it doesn't. Darkness is a good thing when you want to rest, tune out of reality or disconnect from any discomfort or disturbance. But it also involves some risks; you are unable to see obstacles, to see the faces of the people near you or to find an exit to go to into a different space. Darkness can be isolating, and it can also be a trap.

In this passage, Isaiah describes people who have walked and dwelt in a land of deep darkness – so much more problematic than a dark bedroom! This darkness is not simply caused by a light switch; it is a spiritual darkness that has stifled the life of an entire nation of people. But somehow, things change. Isaiah writes that these people have seen a great light, which has shone on them. What is this light and where has it come from? This is a prophetic vision of Christ, the light of the world, who appears to us through the incarnation. We too are those who have walked and dwelt in darkness, and we need this light to awaken us to God, to who we are in him and to who we can be to others. The great light of Christ dispels the darkness in our hearts, in our relationships and in creation.

Lord, thank you for the light of Christ, who has come into our world and abides with us through the Holy Spirit. May we be lights where we are, determined to push back the darkness that stifles the life of your creation.

SELINA STONE

A promised future

Righteousness shall be the belt of his waist, and faithfulness the belt of his loins. The wolf shall dwell with the lamb, and the leopard shall lie down with the young goat, and the calf and the lion and the fattened calf together; and a little child shall lead them. (ESV)

Nowadays, it seems that even within Christian circles we are cautioned against being idealistic, and instead instructed to aim for what is reasonable. The irony of course is that there isn't too much emphasis on what is reasonable in the realm of faith. In this Christmas season, we are asked to believe some totally unreasonable things: that a virgin conceived a son, that angels came to talk to people and most of all that God was born as a human.

The image that Isaiah paints here is another call to believe what seems unreasonable. Talking about Jesus as the one who defines righteousness and faithfulness, Isaiah describes this new world Christ has come to establish in fantastical terms. Anyone who has been to a zoo or watched any nature documentary will be certain that there is no way a wolf and lamb can hang out together without one of them meeting a sticky end. It is totally unrealistic to think that a leopard and young goat or a lion and fattened (tasty) calf could be friends – the basic instincts of one would put the other in mortal danger.

This picture becomes even more incredible, ending as it does with a child leading them all. Isaiah helps us to understand that this Messiah has come to bring about a reality we have never experienced before – where nature itself is transformed in such a way that death and suffering are eradicated, and life and the flourishing of all creation are eternal. This is a vision of hope for the entire world, for people, animals and the soil, for the trees and even for a little child whose future depends on it.

Lord, we thank you that you call us to believe and you give us the grace to hope for the impossible. We thank you for your plan of restoration for our world, and we pray that you will allow us to do our part.

SELINA STONE

A kingdom of hope

'He has brought down the mighty from their thrones and exalted those of humble estate; he has filled the hungry with good things, and the rich he has sent away empty.' (ESV)

The birth of Jesus is astounding for many reasons. We often acknowledge that the incarnation is a miraculous moment of God making his home among us by taking on human form. We know that through his life, death and resurrection, Christ brings about the salvation of all people by restoring us to relationship with God. But this moment is also wonderful because of what it means for those who find themselves forgotten and neglected, for the humble and the hungry.

Throughout Jesus' life, he constantly leans towards those whom no one else is interested in: those on the margins such as prostitutes, the sick, those weighed down by poverty and lack of opportunity, any person ostracised by religion as well as society. Here, before Jesus has even grown into the man who would be this Saviour, Mary catches a prophetic vision of what God is up to and it is much bigger than she may previously have realised. While Mary may identify within her own story of God exalting the humble and filling the hungry with good things, this is not just about her. Jesus will declare a kingdom just like this – where the poor inherit, and it is hard for the rich to enter; where those who hunger are filled and those who seem to have it all do not receive anything.

Mary is one person whose humble obedience to God becomes a sign of things to come, of a whole kingdom where thrones are given to the humble instead of the mighty. Mary is the mother of the King of this kingdom, and her prophetic pronouncement heralds his reign.

All of us have areas where we may be tempted to elevate ourselves rather than to trust God. How do Mary's words and her example inspire you to respond to God and to life's circumstances differently today?

SELINA STONE

The cost of the promise

And Simeon blessed them and said to Mary his mother, 'Behold, this child is appointed for the fall and rising of many in Israel, and for a sign that is opposed (and a sword will pierce through your own soul also), so that thoughts from many hearts may be revealed.' (ESV)

No one wants to hear that a loved one, let alone their child, will face opposition or trouble in life. We all know somewhere in the back of our minds that trouble may come but we hope that by a miracle they might avoid it. For some, it is an illness or a disability that causes their life to be a constant struggle, or some element of their identity for which they may face persecution or discrimination. Either way, knowing in advance that your loved one will suffer, and by extension what your pain will be, is nothing short of heartbreaking.

Here, the prophet tells Mary that Jesus will face great opposition because his ministry will result in a reshuffling of power in Israel. What's more, she will also go through great pain herself. It seems that the cost of obedience to God keeps on mounting for this young woman. Maybe she wondered what her life would have been if the angel had got lost that day, and her life had gone on as normal. The favour of God of which the angels spoke has not led her to a place of a perfectly happy existence, but to a rollercoaster of intense joy and overwhelming agony, and everything in between.

If we carry in our hearts the subtle expectation that when we walk with God, he takes away what is difficult, then Christ's life and that of his mother Mary demonstrate the opposite. This journey involves deep pain, and with it the forming of our character into the image of Christ, who was obedient even unto death.

Take a moment to consider where you may have experienced this sword that pierces the soul in your own journey. Offer up your pain to God in prayer honestly and allow him to speak his healing words of life to you.

SELINA STONE

The promise of justice

The Spirit of the Lord God is upon me, because the Lord has anointed me to bring good news to the poor; he has sent me to bind up the broken-hearted, to proclaim liberty to the captives, and the opening of the prison to those who are bound; to proclaim the year of the Lord's favour. (ESV)

So why has this baby been born and why has this Messiah come? We will see later on in the story that many ideas and expectations are put on Jesus as he grows older. Some want him to be a political revolutionary; others think he is demon-possessed; Satan tempts him to gain power through idolatry; and others find him to be a heretic. However, this baby we have journeyed with grows to be a man who is very clear about why he has come. He is a student of the scriptures and full of the Spirit, learning from religious teachers and growing in faith and knowledge of God. He understands that his purpose is not to please people but to be obedient to the voice of his Father.

We know that these words of Isaiah are about Jesus, because Jesus himself quotes them in the temple in Luke 4 when he begins his ministry. He knows that the Spirit of God is upon him, and that God has called him. He is clear that he has not come for his own fame or success but because he has a mission to serve those who find themselves suffering because of sin and oppression. Christ has come to fulfil a promise that involves the liberation of those who are trapped in poverty, broken-heartedness and all kinds of prisons, both physical and otherwise.

The birth of the Messiah is a sign of God's favour, which is for all people. This salvation leads us to freedom in its truest sense, through the Spirit of the God who made us. The voice of Christ calls us to be his followers, to receive his good news and his salvation, and to be a sign to the world that he has come.

Lord, we thank you for this year and we offer to you everything that it has held for us. May we enter the next year having received your liberty in our hearts and lives, and determined to see the liberation of those who suffer.

SELINA STONE

Day by Day with God is on Instagram!

Follow us for a daily quote from *Day by Day with God*,
to help you meet with God in the everyday.

 Follow us: @daybydaywithgod

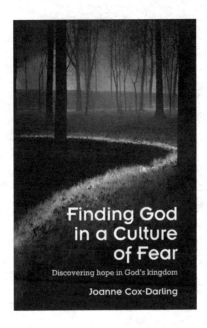

This book takes us beyond comfort zones and easy answers, and towards a deeper understanding and practice of hope. It offers reflections, stories and practical ways for individuals and groups to find hope in their lives through discovering more about God in their midst.

Finding God in a Culture of Fear
Discovering hope in God's kingdom
Joanne Cox-Darling
978 0 85746 646 4 £8.99
brfonline.org.uk

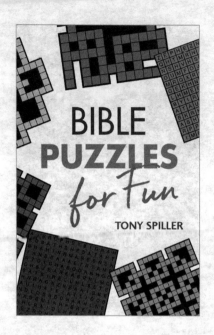

84 puzzles – crosswords, anagrams, word searches, mazes, spirals and others – will make you puzzle over the Bible, increase your biblical knowledge and give you hours of fun. Be ready for some surprises on the way!

Bible Puzzles for Fun
Tony Spiller
978 0 85746 692 1 £8.99
brfonline.org.uk

To order

Online: **brfonline.org.uk**
Telephone: +44 (0)1865 319700
Mon–Fri 9.15–17.30

Delivery times within the UK are normally 15 working days. Prices are correct at the time of going to press but may change without prior notice.

Title	Price	Qty	Total
Finding God in a Culture of Fear	£8.99		
Bible Puzzles for Fun	£8.99		
Day by Day with God (Sep–Dec 2019) – single copy	£4.60		
Day by Day with God (Jan–Apr 2020) – single copy	£4.60		

POSTAGE AND PACKING CHARGES			
Order value	UK	Europe	Rest of world
Under £7.00	£2.00	£5.00	£7.00
£7.00–£29.99	£3.00	£9.00	£15.00
£30.00 and over	FREE	£9.00 + 15% of order value	£15.00 + 20% of order value

Total value of books	
Postage and packing	
Total for this order	

Please complete in BLOCK CAPITALS

Title .... First name/initials .... Surname ....

Address ....

.... Postcode ....

Acc. No. .... Telephone ....

Email ....

Method of payment

❏ Cheque (made payable to BRF) ❏ MasterCard / Visa credit / Visa debit

Card no. ☐☐☐☐ ☐☐☐☐ ☐☐☐☐ ☐☐☐☐ ☐☐☐☐

Expires end ☐☐ ☐☐ Security code* ☐☐☐ Last 3 digits on the reverse of the card

Signature* .... Date .... /............ /............

*ESSENTIAL IN ORDER TO PROCESS YOUR ORDER

Please return this form to:
BRF, 15 The Chambers, Vineyard, Abingdon OX14 3FE | enquiries@brf.org.uk
To read our terms and find out about cancelling your order, please visit **brfonline.org.uk/terms**.

The Bible Reading Fellowship (BRF) is a Registered Charity (233280)

SUBSCRIPTION INFORMATION

Each issue of *Day by Day with God* is available from Christian bookshops everywhere. Copies may also be available through your church book agent or from the person who distributes Bible reading notes in your church.

Alternatively you may obtain *Day by Day with God* on subscription direct from the publishers. There are two kinds of subscription:

Individual subscriptions
covering 3 issues for 4 copies or less, payable in advance (including postage & packing).

To order, please complete the details on page 144 and return with the appropriate payment to: BRF, 15 The Chambers, Vineyard, Abingdon OX14 3FE

You can also use the form on page 144 to order a gift subscription for a friend.

Group subscriptions
covering 3 issues for 5 copies or more, sent to one UK address (post free).

Please note that the annual billing period for group subscriptions runs from 1 May to 30 April.

To order, please complete the details on page 143 and return with the appropriate payment to: BRF, 15 The Chambers, Vineyard, Abingdon OX14 3FE

You will receive an invoice with the first issue of notes.

All our Bible reading notes can be ordered
online by visiting **biblereadingnotes.org.uk/
subscriptions**

Day by Day with God is also available as
an app for Android, iPhone and iPad
biblereadingnotes.org.uk/apps

All subscription enquiries should be directed to:
BRF, 15 The Chambers, Vineyard, Abingdon OX14 3FE
+44 (0)1865 319700 | enquiries@brf.org.uk

DBDWG0319

DAY BY DAY WITH GOD GROUP SUBSCRIPTION FORM

All our Bible reading notes can be ordered online by visiting
biblereadingnotes.org.uk/subscriptions

The group subscription rate for *Day by Day with God* will be £13.80 per person until April 2020.

☐ I would like to take out a group subscription for .... (quantity) copies.

☐ Please start my order with the January 2020 / May 2020 / September 2020* issue. I would like to pay annually/receive an invoice* with each edition of the notes. (*delete as appropriate)

Please do not send any money with your order. Send your order to BRF and we will send you an invoice. The group subscription year is from 1 May to 30 April. If you start subscribing in the middle of a subscription year we will invoice you for the remaining number of issues left in that year.

Name and address of the person organising the group subscription:

Title .... First name/initials .... Surname ....

Address ....

.... Postcode ....

Telephone .... Email ....

Church ....

Name of Minister ....

Name and address of the person paying the invoice if the invoice needs to be sent directly to them:

Title .... First name/initials .... Surname ....

Address ....

.... Postcode ....

Telephone .... Email ....

Please return this form to:
BRF, 15 The Chambers, Vineyard, Abingdon OX14 3FE | **enquiries@brf.org.uk**

To read our terms and find out about cancelling your order,
please visit **brfonline.org.uk/terms**.

The Bible Reading Fellowship is a Registered Charity (233280)

DAY BY DAY WITH GOD INDIVIDUAL/GIFT SUBSCRIPTION FORM

To order online, please visit **biblereadingnotes.org.uk/subscriptions**

☐ I would like to give a gift subscription (please provide both names and addresses)

☐ I would like to take out a subscription myself (complete your name and address details only once)

Title _____ First name/initials _____ Surname _____

Address _____

_____ Postcode _____

Telephone _____ Email _____

Gift subscription name _____

Gift subscription address _____

_____ Postcode _____

Gift subscription (20 words max. or include your own gift card):

_____

_____

Please send *Day by Day with God* beginning with the January 2020 / May 2020 / September 2020 issue (*delete as appropriate*):

(please tick box)	UK	Europe	Rest of world
1-year subscription	☐ £17.40	☐ £25.50	☐ £29.40
2-year subscription	☐ £33.00	N/A	N/A

Total enclosed £ _____ (cheques should be made payable to 'BRF')

Please charge my MasterCard / Visa credit / Visa debit with £ _____

Card no. ☐☐☐☐ ☐☐☐☐ ☐☐☐☐ ☐☐☐☐

Expires end ☐☐☐☐ Security code* ☐☐☐ Last 3 digits on the reverse of the card

Signature* _____ Date _____/_____/_____

*ESSENTIAL IN ORDER TO PROCESS YOUR ORDER

Please return this form to:
BRF, 15 The Chambers, Vineyard, Abingdon OX14 3FE | enquiries@brf.org.uk

To read our terms and find out about cancelling your order, please visit **brfonline.org.uk/terms**.   The Bible Reading Fellowship is a Registered Charity (233280)

DBDWG0319